Zen and the Art of Dealing with Difficult People

Zen and the Art of Dealing with Difficult People

Mark Westmoquette

Foreword by Julian Daizan Skinner

WATKINS

Sharing Wisdom Since 1893

Zen and the Art of Dealing with Difficult People
Mark Westmoquette

First published in the UK and USA in 2021 by
Watkins, an imprint of Watkins Media Limited
Unit 11, Shepperton House, 83–93 Shepperton Road
London N1 3DF

enquiries@watkinspublishing.com

Commissioning Editor: Fiona Robertson
Editor: Steve Marshall
Editorial Assistant: Brittany Willis
Head of Design: Glen Wilkins
Production: Uzma Taj

A CIP record for this book is available from the British Library

ISBN: 978-1-78678-548-0 (Paperback)
ISBN: 978-1-78678-610-4 (eBook)

10 9 8 7 6 5 4 3 2 1

Typeset by Lapiz

Printed in the United Kingdom by TJ Books Ltd

www.watkinspublishing.com

I tell everyone that just as they say that children are mirrors to their parents, so too all those one comes in contact with are your own mirrors. Therefore, if you give all your heart and try your best to communicate, you are sure to get a similar response. So, please lead a life in which you think of what you can do for others, not what others can do for you. Interact with others by trying to give all your heart and doing your best to communicate.[1]

(Japanese Tendai Buddhist Monk Mitsunaga Kakudo)

CONTENTS

FOREWORD

Buddhas appear troublesomely; ancestors teach in detail.

(Keizan)[2]

As a young Zen monk, my life was pressed against others. There was nowhere to hide. For seven years I lived in a one-mat space in the monastery meditation hall surrounded by twenty fellow monks. There we meditated, slept and sometimes ate. The life was designed to be stripped of distractions. The training process was compared to a rock tumbler. The inevitable interpersonal manifestations of selfishness were expected to grind against each other, the idea being that we novices would enter as rough pebbles and emerge as polished jewels. Sometimes feelings ran high. The only time I've ever chased someone with murder in my mind was during this period. In our little world there were a number of attempted suicides and one that went all the way.

Most often, however, the outcome was very different. I have seen for myself psychologically well-adjusted, unselfish and luminous human beings emerge from this abrasion. The essence of the work was clarity and awareness. When leavened with generosity of spirit, humour and compassion, transformation could be rapid. The quotation above, a rather free translation from the work of Japanese Zen master Keizan (1268–1325), was frequently cited by our teachers.

Your troublesome Buddha is the person who presses your buttons, bringing up sensitivities and irritation, jealousy, inadequacy or other buried miscontents. No suffering can be dealt with in the abstract. It is only as these things arise into consciousness that we have the opportunity to resolve them.

The key to the transformation is to recognize the opportunity in the pain. It's so easy to blame the other person, to blame the past, to blame the system and, speaking personally, a lot of the time that's precisely what I did. It's also possible to blame yourself, even to deny the presence of such unworthy antisocial feelings.

But Zen monastery life is set up to make any of these stances unsustainable. Eventually, all being well, the trainee starts to "turn the light around" – to be present with the pain, to give it an arena of non-judgemental, non-reactive awareness. In this compassionate awareness the physical, energetic, emotional and mental dimensions of the suffering begin to untwist and will eventually "re-integrate" (to use the Jungian term) into a new harmonious relationship with the whole.

None of this can happen without the initial suffering arising. Hence that difficult person is actually the true teacher, the Buddha, of the moment. And what of the teaching in detail? Subjectively, the process can feel quite relentless. Until the hot button is fully dealt with, the associated pain will arise and arise. Perhaps it's natural to think of spiritual life as a withdrawal from the distractions and drama of our humanity. This withdrawal is certainly possible. For example, after his own enlightenment beneath the Bodhi Tree, the Buddha was faced with a choice. He could remain, enjoying the fruits of his quest in peace and solitude, becoming a *pratyekabuddha* – a silent Buddha. Or he could get up from his sitting place and begin the tiresome work of training others to confront their suffering. The fact that he is remembered reveals the Buddha's choice and the compassionate spirit that looks beyond individual benefit.

It seems that from his earliest days of teaching, the Buddha strongly promoted the ideal of *sangha* – spiritual fellowship. Furthermore, he defined his teaching as one in which "one does not keep quarrelling with anyone in the cosmos".[3] To this day, disharmony and schism in the *sangha* are considered matters of the gravest importance. Why would this social dimension of practice be so important? According to the so-called "social proximity effect", our nature as group animals determines that we humans inevitably become more like those with whom we spend the most time. But as well as mutual reinforcement and support, the Zen tradition highlights the growth potential of spirited and even dramatic mutual challenge in the *sangha*:

> Once Zen master Obaku (died 850) sent his student Rinzai to deliver a letter to another Zen master's monastery.
>
> At that time Gyosan was guest master. He took the letter and asked: "This letter is from Obaku; but his special messenger, what has he to do with it?"
>
> Rinzai immediately slapped him.
>
> Gyosan stopped him and said: "Elder brother, since you know about this matter, let's cease."[4]

After his study of the old Zen records unexpectedly revealed that most often the student's moment of awakening is prompted by an interaction, our teacher in Japan, Zen master Shinzan, developed a mutual inquiry process that he called "group *sanzen*".[5] Here at Zenways we continue this work in our "Breakthrough to Zen" retreats. I believe one of the most awe-inspiring and beautiful experiences a human being can have is to witness this moment of shift in another.

But practice with others is not just about this elevated level of human development. Alongside his unstinting praise for those within his *sangha* who embodied compassion, love and wisdom, the Buddha, to the end of his life, had to devote tremendous time and energy to dealing with abusive supporters, false accusations of sexual misconduct, even worldly ambition that reached the level of attempted murder. His enlightenment didn't release him from engagement with these realms. And if it's true for the Buddha, it's going to be true for the rest of us. However profound and transforming your inner cultivation becomes, your practice will involve dealing with human soap opera – for life. In whatever sphere you find yourself, your fellow travellers are unlikely to be perfect; your teachers and seniors are unlikely to be perfect; you yourself are unlikely to be perfect.

The atomization of modern life means that for a lay practitioner it's never been easier to just give up on the hard work of human *sangha* interaction in favour of withdrawal. But to do so is to miss out on so much. If we hide out, we're not going to meet these troublesome Buddhas. When I began to teach Zen to myself outside the monastic setting, I wanted to find ways in which students could benefit from the potential of this transformative perspective on practice.

The arenas were not difficult to find. Family life, work life, friendship groups – all contain abundant troublesome Buddhas. In addition, when I was asked to develop a programme for training future Zen teachers, I wanted the students to have ample opportunity to learn through the interpersonal mutual abrasion I'd grown up with. As a *sangha* we created a monastery without walls. Trainee Zen teachers work with me (more than one person has called me "the skinner") as well as with the rawness and roughness of their peers.

Some time ago, Mark Kuren Westmoquette and I were sitting together and discussing this dimension of Zen practice. He tells me that that particular conversation was the seed of this book. Perhaps Mark's own story is illustrative of what can happen. More than a dozen years ago, he came to me a shy, awkward astrophysicist. Even holding eye contact was difficult for him. The product of a painful and difficult childhood, Mark had come to realize that the abstract world of high science had attracted him because it was safely distanced from the human pain and messiness of the social world. He was equally clear that this distancing was not serving him and was quietly determined to find another way.

Becoming an active member of the Zenways practice community, Mark experienced and witnessed many of the interpersonal stresses and growth opportunities he details in the text here. At the same time he worked intensively with the troublesome Buddhas in his family and in the ultra-competitive world of academia.

In 2009 he began his training to be a Zen yoga teacher, finding in the training a first connection with the energy and bliss of mindful embodied practice and the power of building deep connections with other people.

Over time, Mark found his life shifting. He had faced and transformed so much pain within himself. Now a deep wish to be primarily orientated toward people rather than distant stars led him to move into teaching Zen meditation and yoga full-time, working as a hospital chaplain, running Zen practice groups for populations in the prison and homelessness spheres and working with me intensively as my assistant.

His practice bore great fruit in 2010 on a retreat at my teacher's temple, Gyokuryuji, in central Japan. Zen master Shinzan pulled me aside between meditation periods and whispered four words in English: "Red hair open eye." Mark, who had red hair, had entered the gate of *kensho*, the Zen term meaning "awakening to your true nature".

Following a period of him maturing and developing his practice, including a spell as an ordained Zen monk wandering the lanes of Britain living on alms food, I named Mark a Zen teacher in 2015.

Over the years Mark's interpersonal confidence and presence had grown. He became able to date and eventually get married. Bringing together his explorations of the outer and inner universes, he wrote a couple of books, *Mindful Thoughts for Stargazers* and *The Mindful Universe*. After 12 years of Zen training, largely amid the hurly-burly of *sangha* interactions, he took some time during a two-year retreat period on a remote island in the South Atlantic to reflect on this vital human dimension of spiritual practice and write this book.

Mark mentioned to me that he was keen to highlight and honour the work of others in our Zenways practice community, many of whom have been willing to share their interpersonal struggles and learnings in these pages.

If you have an interest in contemplative practice, there's a tiny chance that you are one of the thousand or so complete hermits in the world. Otherwise you have a place in the human matrix of troublesome Buddhas. If that is the case, this book is for you. Here you'll find a sure and practical guide to transforming the lead of human frictions into the gold of a love that embraces all of yourself, all beings and the entire universe.

Wishing you abundant Buddhas along your way.

Julian Daizan Skinner
Zenways London Dojo
Rohatsu 2020

INTRODUCTION

We all encounter troublesome or challenging people in our lives. They drive us up the wall, irritate the hell out of us and even prompt us to think dreadful thoughts. It might be your colleague, your downstairs neighbour, your partner or your mum, or any number of people we encounter on a regular basis, or perhaps just once.

Our language is full of colourful metaphors describing what these people do to us. We say things like "they pushed my buttons", "they grate on me", "they get on my wick", "they're a pain in the neck", "they rub me up the wrong way" or "we're just not on the same wavelength". What is it about these people that causes such discomfort? And how do we work with this discomfort so that it doesn't escalate and cause more discomfort? In this book we'll be examining a variety of situations in life where troublesome people can show up; we'll explore how the teachings of Zen and mindfulness can help. Ultimately, these teachings will show us how the most troublesome people can become our best teachers. We'll learn how we can see each of them as beautiful, unique expressions of this one universe to which we all belong – we'll see their Buddha-nature.

In my experience, people have a view of Zen as a tradition of profound stillness, calmness, patience and simplicity, and expect Zen practitioners to embody these characteristics at all times. Even after more than a decade of practice, I can tell you I don't exude profound stillness all the time – in fact not even much of the time! It's possible that one day I will – but as far as I understand it, that's not actually what Zen is about. Zen is about finding your true nature and, once you've woken up to it, learning to live from that realization. But even in that place of realization (which we'll explore in detail as we go on), there will always be people who get up your nose – and perhaps even make your blood boil and steam come out of your ears. Zen teaches us how to listen to those feelings and begin relating to them in a different way.

Who is this book for?

This book is for anyone wanting to learn how to respond to difficult people and situations with more clarity and wisdom. You might be someone who has a number of troublesome people in various quarters of your life, or perhaps you have one particularly enraging one, or you have brushed up against an array of them at different points in your life. You can see that there's often a pattern to your behaviour in relation to them and it usually causes pain – perhaps a great deal of pain. The only way we can grow is by facing this pain, acknowledging how we feel and how we've reacted, and making a commitment to end this repeating pattern of suffering. In this book, I assume no previous experience with mindfulness or Zen (or indeed any kind of Buddhism), and by no means do you need to identify as a Buddhist or adhere to any beliefs.

I remember when I first started practising Zen, my teacher told me to treat it like a scientific experiment. The lab was my body and mind, and although the methodology had been refined over many centuries, the result and conclusions were up to me to find. There was no correct answer – just my answer. At this point in my life, I was about 20 years old, studying for a degree in astrophysics and really appreciated this pragmatic approach. I, of course, had my head buried in equations and intellectual learning and had for some years really struggled to connect to my emotional side. I can now see that part of the reason for choosing such a subject – which is intellectual and focused on things as far removed from Earth and real life as you can get – was that I was trying to escape.

Who am I to talk to you about how to deal with troublesome people?

When I was 13, my mum and stepdad were in a car accident that killed my stepdad and put my mum into hospital with first-degree burns over most of her body. The person who caused the accident was an off-duty police officer who had been racing his friend along the road. In a misjudged moment he clipped the front of my mum's car, causing it to spin out of control across the road and crash head-on into another car, bursting into flames. To save my mum's life they amputated both her legs and one arm. This happened seven years after my biological father was expelled from our family home. When I was six my mum found out he had been sexually abusing me and my sister.

During my life I've had my fair share of particularly challenging individuals to deal with. My father and the off-duty policeman who caused my mum's accident have been two that stand out. With them, it's taken many years of practice and deep enquiry to get to a place where I can see past the horrific things they did. I can now see them as people with their own suffering, and their deeds have shown me so much about myself and the very nature of being human (as I'll discuss in Part 4). But I've also come across many garden-variety troublesome people: for many years I had an office job and I can certainly remember one or two difficult office-mates; I spent years commuting in London alongside various irksome fellow travellers and I lived in a few house-shares with a good number of vexing housemates. I have also been in a romantic relationship with someone for ten years (the last five of which we've been married). As wonderful as that's been, boy has it brought up some troublesome situations through which I've learnt and grown a great deal!

Learning how to see life's troublesome people as my best teachers has by no means been a quick or easy learning process, or something I've done alone. In writing this book I've benefitted from the wisdom of a number of enlightened people. As well as practising Zen in a community with a Zen master for over a decade and practising yoga over a period of 20 years with a handful of fantastic teachers, I also spent three and a half years seeing a psychotherapist. A central thread running through these areas of development has been the practice of mindfulness.

At its root, mindfulness is a technique for perceiving things clearly, letting things be and letting things go. The clarity we gain through seeing things just as they are gives us the critical information we need to make wise choices about how we act next. This is one of the key skills to develop when working with difficult people.

I wouldn't like to say that I've got it all figured out. It seems important to approach the challenging questions we shall explore in this book with a healthy dose of "I don't know". I still get irritated and angry with people and fail to appreciate both their own suffering and their interconnectedness to the whole universe. I'm a work in progress – as we all shall be until the day we die.

Finding a teacher in the car park

So how exactly can we come to see a troublesome person as our best teacher? It sounds crazy! Let's take a concrete example. You're in a car park manoeuvring to get into a parking space, then someone nips in there before you and pretends they haven't seen you. A normal impulsive reaction (one made without conscious choice) might be to shout, curse and then consider scratching a key along their car to punish them. How could this person possibly teach you anything except how not to behave? And how can you get to a place where you can perceive their intrinsic good nature and see them as not separate from you? It sounds like a tall order. It is – but not an impossible one. The first step is to develop a genuine willingness to examine how you relate to this difficult parking-space stealer.

An initial reaction might be one of anger – they're being selfish by taking something that was yours (the parking space), and by not acknowledging you they're implying you don't matter – or worse, you don't exist. These thoughts comprising your initial stance all arise out of a hard distinction between "that person" and "you". However, if we can bring a sincere awareness and an open enquiry to how we feel, then this initial stance will necessarily begin to shift to something much broader and more inclusive. First, we can acknowledge that our own habits, past experiences and suffering contribute to our reactions. Perhaps you were in a rush already, or excited to get where you were going. Perhaps you were struggling to manoeuvre into the space and were already slightly frustrated. Perhaps the type of car they're driving added energy to the reaction because you already held some prejudiced beliefs about what kind of person owns that car. Was it really "your" space in the first place? Perhaps they really didn't see you.

None of these suggestions are meant to excuse a person who maliciously took your space, but by simply asking the questions we immediately begin softening our position. Thus, the ways in which we act or think impulsively can show us where we are stuck, and where our old patterns and habits are playing out. More than that, by softening our stance, we can start to see beyond the irritating behaviour to the person behind it – a person with their own habits, past experiences and personal suffering. They might have been in a terrible rush – perhaps they were called in to pick up a sick family member, or late for a job interview. Perhaps they've developed a self-protective way-of-being in response to something that's happened in their life. Perhaps they've had the kind of life that has encouraged selfish behaviour. We just don't know.

As our standpoint relaxes and our view expands, we become less reactive to the irritation. Sure, the feeling is still there, perhaps as intense as ever, but we are no longer holding on so much to these emotions and acting on them. Slowly and gradually, we can soften further. We may even start to feel gratitude toward that other person for showing us – teaching us – where we instinctively put up our defences and react out of a feeling of separation, a sense of what "they" are doing to "me", and what "I" deserve. This is a place from which, if we're truly honest and open with ourselves, we have an opportunity to accept, soften, grow and heal. Like this, every challenging situation or encounter with a troublesome person is transformed into an opportunity for us to act with greater wisdom and compassion.

More than that, the seeds of wisdom, compassion and gratitude can grow into a totally new view of the people who irritate or anger you. Conventional understanding is that you and that person or people are separate. We say: "This is me and here is my 'edge', and that is you" or "I'm this kind of person and you're that kind of person". This type of thinking arises from the perspective of separation and discrimination. However, Zen points out that these fixed, separate worldviews represent only one side of how things are.

The experience of awakening (or enlightenment) is the process of seeing and experiencing the other perspective – that life is fluid, dynamic, constantly changing, and that we are all just transitory emanations of the universe in this moment. As my Zen teacher would say: "Rather than being a thing in a world of things, we see we are a process in a world of processes." The way I've come to understand these two viewpoints is by imagining a mountain range enveloped in a cloud with the rocky peaks protruding through the top of the veil. We see these peaks as separate, distinct and pretty much permanent – like the concepts of you and me, or objects like the wall or table. But when the clouds clear away, we see how the mountaintops are connected to one other via the valley floors. The mountains are all part of the one range – equivalently you and I, the wall and table, are all connected and just different parts of the whole.

And they're not really permanent. They change (albeit very slowly in the case of mountains).

From this non-separate viewpoint, that person who angered you is as separate from you as your left hand is from the right. You and they co-create the situation together. Like you, they are temporary manifestations of this one universe. In Zen, seeing them like this is called seeing their Buddha-nature. But it doesn't matter what you call it – their luminous being, their true nature – it means the same thing. They are a Buddha appearing troublesomely.

What this book will and won't cover

This book will take a mindful approach to the problems of dealing with various difficult people. The practice of mindfulness involves allowing whatever arises to be fully seen and acknowledged; we do our best not to value it as good or bad, think it's the way it should or shouldn't be or see it as something we do or don't want. In mindfulness, we're not fundamentally concerned with the content of what comes to our attention – who said what, the whys and wherefores and the storylines of any individual situation. What matters is our relationship to those things that arise. As such, I won't be giving step-by-step advice on how to deal with particular cases and situations, but will provide you with the tools to work out for yourself the best course of action. However, if a troublesome person's behaviour ever escalates to the level of abuse, I would encourage you to reach out and speak to someone (perhaps a professional) who can help in your immediate situation.

This book will aim to steer you away from simply listing all your complaints and grievances. Complaining and generally moaning about our life can feel cathartic, but if we give our gripes attention (and thus energy) without considering what we might do about them, then we are just watering the seeds of negativity. Without giving all the emotional energy of frustration and anger that arises from our complaints a positive, constructive, wholesome avenue to go down, they will inevitably manifest unwisely or even destructively.

I'll show you ways to broaden and soften your stance, find kindness and encourage insights to arise about yourself and your relationship to the world around you. As a result, you will find ways of seeing the essential true nature of everyone you encounter, whether they be troublesome or easy people.

Where we'll go next

In Part 1, we'll explore the question of how life's difficult people can become our teachers. The foundational stones of this process are mindfulness and attunement – without a keen awareness of how we're feeling and what we're doing, and how others are feeling, there's no hope of changing the way we relate to difficult people and learning from these encounters. We'll look at why it is that, in the face of a troublesome person, we find it difficult to maintain emotional regulation – the ability to control our behaviour, keep our temper in check and avoid saying or doing something regretful. I'll posit that the two main things that can pull us out of regulation are the activation of our threat response (causing our defences to rise and our perception to narrow) and the chaos of emotions that can ensue (which can overwhelm us and tangle together to the point of obscuring our view).

Bringing genuine awareness and kindness to challenging relationships is difficult, and requires courage, patience and compassion. We'll discuss why being honestly open to our experiences is so important, however difficult, painful or confusing it is. Ultimately, emotions are important messengers, and if we repress or ignore them, or aren't able to fully acknowledge them, we'll lose touch with what's really going on. We'll then discuss how we can restore emotional regulation, both when we're alone and in the safe company of trusted others.

Besides losing it now and then in the heat of the moment, each of us has a generally preferred pattern of coping and responding to relationship difficulties. Some get angry, others withdraw and others always try and smooth the situation to avoid potential conflict. Thus our troublesome encounters can also teach us a great deal about our general attitudes and habits. In discussing these behavioural traits, I'll introduce a number of examples and unpack some Zen koans (spiritual questions or stories) that will help point us toward some of the areas we can get stuck in and how we can unstick ourselves.

Lastly we'll explore how important it is to be compassionate. As we begin seeing and acknowledging the way we are around troublesome people, and how our past experiences and suffering contribute to our reactions, it's critical we apply that compassion to ourselves as much as to anyone else.

Part 2 includes a wide variety of inspiring stories of how different people have encountered challenging people in various arenas of life and found deep lessons from their experience. We'll look at examples from the workplace, in friendship networks, at home in the form of partners, spouses or other members of the family, in the form of neighbours and housemates and in the wider world in the form of fellow travellers. We'll also look at how role models and teachers, and in particular spiritual teachers, can become troublesome Buddhas, and what that might bring to light about ourselves.

Part 3 focuses on the far end of the troublesome spectrum, on learning how to deal with those people who have abused us or caused us profound pain in some way. I'll introduce you to a couple of ogre figures that have featured in my own life and how I've learnt a great deal about myself through examining my relationship with them. We'll also explore another troublesome person – the self. Although much of what this book is about revolves around our self and how we relate to who we are, in this part I'll draw out a few additional areas to explore.

However difficult, irritating or malicious, no one is a distinct entity existing in and of themselves. We are all different facets of this one universe – dynamic and interconnected like waves on the ocean. This is the area we'll be exploring in Part 4. Perceiving other people as equal manifestations of this one universe, each with the potential to wake up to this perspective, is called seeing their true nature or Buddha-nature. However, perceiving is only one half of the equation. The last element we'll explore is how it might be to act from this realization – to respond spontaneously to difficult people from the recognition of both their suffering and innate Buddha-nature.

PART ONE

TROUBLESOME PEOPLE AS OUR TEACHERS

CHAPTER 1
MINDFULNESS AND ATTUNEMENT

I'd like to make it clear at this point that this book is not about how to rid your life of troublesome people. No matter how enlightened you get, there will always be people that grate on you and rub you up the wrong way. This book is also not about simply learning to tolerate troublesome people. Turning ourselves into the universe's door mat and letting people get away with hurtful behaviour is not kind to ourselves – or indeed kind to those people. This book is about how the troublesome people in our lives can show us where we can develop and grow as human beings. The first part of this book in particular is about how we can let encounters with troublesome people illuminate areas within ourselves that are hidden, in pain, acting through old habits or otherwise holding on. Once we start becoming aware of these things we can begin responding to troublesome people with more wisdom.

Imagine you're on a ship on the ocean and wanting to sail to a particular port. If you're not sure where you are, it doesn't matter what direction you take – you'll never get to the port. The crucial first step is to work out where you are. When it comes to navigating the stormy seas of troublesome relationships, mindfulness is a critical skill. It's what allows us to plot our current position. Mindfulness means bringing deliberate awareness to what's happening in this moment. It's our way of working out where we are on the map – noticing sensations, body posture, thoughts, memories and ideas – so we can make an informed decision about what direction we're going to take next.

What's also important is *how* we perceive what we become aware of – how we go about plotting our position on the map. It's possible to bring a detached, cold and judgemental awareness to what we notice – a bit like being a CCTV camera. This kind of awareness can easily exacerbate the troublesomeness of the relationship because of the myriad judgements and criticisms we make. But it's also possible to bring an embodied, warm and compassionate awareness to what we find. This means having a friendly, gentle and open attitude, where we do our utmost not to judge what we find to be good or bad – or, in fact, wish it were any different in that moment. Having an awareness with this kind of caring intent toward ourselves is called self-attunement – metaphorically sitting down, putting an arm around ourselves and tuning in to what we feel. This is the true practice of mindfulness.

Since emotional pain and tension originates in the body, in the teachings of mindfulness there's a strong emphasis on directing awareness toward the physical aspect of our inner experience – noticing the body's orientation and posture, and the sensations that are arising within it. This is important because we must get to know our body and understand how it sees and reacts to the world if we're to wisely navigate any kind of troublesome relationship.

Although we can all be mindful at times, mindfulness is a skill that we can develop. We can become more mindful, more of the time, if we practise. When I first started Zen meditation, I was barely able to hold my attention for a few seconds on something as simple and unthreatening as my breath, let alone something more charged – like, for example, the gamut of complex feelings that arose when I started to get angry with someone. Staying mindful when things get heated or emotional is something that needs building up to. That's why it's best to start by developing the skills of compassionate awareness in comfortable (or at least neutral) situations.

Thus to begin with, try practising mindfulness with an easy body posture, in a quiet and non-threatening space with as few distractions as possible. Pay close attention to what's happening in the moment with care. Non-judgement and honesty must become a habit – something we do frequently when we're nowhere near troublesome people or emotional stimulation. Let's try a simple practice now. If you don't do anything like this regularly already, I'd suggest doing this every day to start building up your skills of honest awareness, attention, patience and kindness.

Practice: mindfulness of the body and sensations

Arrange your body into a comfortable, upright sitting posture. Make sure your spine is long, balanced and aligned with your chin tucked in a little so the back of your neck is long. Let your gaze rest on these words. Let go of any tension in your face and shoulders. Relax into your belly.

Start to direct your attention inward. During this practice you may notice certain sensations that aren't pleasant – perhaps painful, uncomfortable, awkward, heavy, constricted or chaotic. Simply do your best to notice whatever is there without judging it to be good or bad, or something you want or don't want. It's not always easy, but do your best.

First, bring your attention to your head. Notice its weight – is it leaning to one side? There's no right or wrong, just notice. How does it feel inside your head? Tight, spacious, heavy, light? What can you feel in your forehead? Your eyelids, cheeks, jaw, lips, chin? If there's any tension or tightness, that's fine – just let it be and notice if it changes. If there are very few or no sensations, that's also fine. If you find yourself visualizing the body parts, just put those thoughts to the side and try to feel those areas from the inside.

If you get distracted (perhaps by reading on down the page or thinking about something else), don't worry. Just return your attention to your body and carry on.

Notice your shoulders. How do they feel? Are they tense, relaxed, up or down? Does the left side feel different to the right? Again, however they are, it's fine. Just notice.

Become aware of your chest … your shoulder blades … your spine – its shape and curves … your lower back.

Notice what you can feel in your belly. Take your time – don't just skim-read these words but really sense inside your belly. Sometimes there are strong sensations, sometimes less so. Sometimes the sensations are subtle, so it may take a little while to notice anything.

Notice your arms – the bend in your elbows … your hands – wherever they are, whatever they're touching: temperature, pressure, the curl of your fingers, how you're holding this page.

Become aware of your hips and pelvis and all the deep layers of muscle and tissue. Notice your thighs … knees … lower legs … ankles, feet and toes. If your feet are in socks and/or shoes, how does that feel?

Now see if you can let your attention broaden out to encompass your whole body. Do you feel generally light or heavy? Warm or cold? Tense or relaxed? Remember, there's no right or wrong, should or shouldn't – however you find your body, right here and now, is your experience. As much as you can, let it be just as it is.

Now take a nice deep breath and have a stretch if you like.

CHAPTER 2
DYSREGULATION – WHY WE LOSE IT WITH DIFFICULT PEOPLE

In order to begin responding more wisely to difficult people, we first need to understand a little more about what happens in our body during a difficult interaction. Under normal, non-troublesome circumstances we are what you could call "emotionally regulated": we feel calm, steady and settled, and are able to manage (consciously or unconsciously) how our emotions influence our behaviour. This means we can start, stop or otherwise temper our emotional responses in a way that's socially acceptable and doesn't evoke stress or fear. Troublesome encounters can easily send us toward emotional dysregulation. That steady, settled feeling dissolves, and we become less and less able to control our behaviour. When this happens we can easily act inappropriately and do or say things that are in opposition to our core values and that we might later regret. If we want to respond wisely to a troublesome person, then it's important we explore why, in a heated situation, it can be difficult to stay on top of our rising emotions and remain regulated.

Threat and neuroception

One of the jobs of our unconscious brain is to assess the level of threat that any given situation or person presents. This threat-assessment sense is known as "neuroception" – a term coined by Dr Stephen Porges, one of the pioneers in the field of stress and trauma.[6] Porges is careful to point out that neuroception operates wholly beneath our conscious awareness – although it is very much conditioned (influenced) by past experiences and beliefs. By taking in all the information presented to it by our senses, the brain's neuroceptive circuits determine whether any given situation or person is safe, dangerous or life-threatening. When it perceives safety, we feel regulated and are able to engage comfortably on a social level. If it perceives danger, the system might mobilize the body in what's known as a "fight or flight" reaction (characterized by a flush of adrenaline, a tightening of the muscles and a narrowing of attention). In common parlance we sometimes say "I flipped my lid" – which, strangely enough, loosely describes what happens on a neurological level. The part of the brain that's responsible for self-reflection, reasoning and making conscious decisions (the front and top of the brain – the lid you might say) becomes overwhelmed by (flips off or disconnects from) the part that deals with our emotional threat response (the limbic centre in the middle of the brain). Hence we become dysregulated. At maximum threat level – in a perceived life-threatening situation – the brain might instead initiate a shut-down or "immobilization" reaction (characterized by the body going limp and the mind disconnecting or going blank – like stage fright). All these reactions are hard-wired into our system by eons of evolution because they've proved rather effective at saving our lives.

However, there's more to our complicated social world than just survival.

Imagine the following scenario: you're cycling down a busy street and someone opens the door of a parked car just a short way ahead. At the sight of this, your body initiates a fight or flight response – your heart rate and blood pressure shoot up, your muscles flush with new blood and your mind becomes single-pointed in its focus – you swerve violently to avoid crashing. A torrent of swear words pour out of your mouth, some of which you thought you'd never use because they're so offensive. The person who opened the door shouts abuse back at you. A little further on, your fists clench and you consider getting off your bike and giving that person what they deserve. In this imagined scenario, the initial fight or flight response was to a genuine physical threat – and it may very well have saved your life. But what happens next determines whether you go home safely or get arrested for attacking the driver.

It's important to know that all of us have neuroceptive circuits that react similarly to any *perceived* threat – whether that's from the outside world (like the door of a parked car) or from the inside world (like thinking that someone doesn't like you). When someone sniggers at a mistake you've made, your body may quickly initiate a fight or flight reaction because your brain sees the laughter as an attack – not on your physical body, but on your sense of identity or self. This is critical to understand when considering difficult people. With its threat-detection circuitry, the brain is always asking, "could I get hurt – on a physical, emotional or even existential level?"

I remember in my second year of university turning up to an exam on quantum mechanics and feeling very much under threat. Despite studying physics, mathematics was never really a strong point of mine. As the exam approached, I started to feel more and more nervous and tense. My brain had perceived a threat – this time to my sense of self. It saw the general threat of being judged and, more specifically, the threat of doing badly in the exam, and had triggered a mild activation of my fight or flight system. I remember involuntarily playing through numerous catastrophic scenarios in my mind, like trying to answer a question and not remembering anything. This rumination only exacerbated my body's fight or flight response – so much so that when I was sitting in the exam hall and the announcement came to turn over the paper and start, I noticed a drip of blood on the desk coming from my nose. Quickly the drip became a torrent and I had to be taken out. And that was before I'd even looked at the exam paper!

Sometimes, instead of a fight or flight (mobilization) response, our neuroception perceives a threat that it doesn't think we can fight or run away from. In this case it's more likely to send the body into shut-down (an immobilization response). Just the other day I was in a meeting with a group of people I don't know very well. On previous occasions I've found this group to be a little cliquey and difficult. When I made a suggestion in response to an issue, one of the group laughed like I'd made a joke, then said something rather condescending. At this, I immediately felt myself withdrawing, both physically and emotionally – a little like a snail retracting its eye-stalks when they touch an obstacle. I felt myself slump just a little more into my chair and I became quieter for the rest of the meeting.

In any threatening situation, the first step to ensuring our behaviour minimizes harm and maximizes kindness is to become aware of our sensations and feelings. The intention is not to change those feelings (it's impossible to change how we feel in that moment), but to modulate, or take conscious control, of what happens next. Without this, our basic survival instincts will take the director's chair and may instigate all sorts of unwise, threat-triggered reactions. So we do our best to bring an openness and curiosity to what we feel in that moment. This awareness provides the conscious mind with information that it can use to make conscious choices as to how we act – in essence, to turn reactions into responses. The more awareness we have, the wiser our responses can become.

So how do we train ourselves to remain aware as the heat rises? First, we need to regularly practise being mindful of our internal world in a comfortable, non-threatening environment. Practise, practise, practise! Then we can apply that understanding to neutral situations, then to increasingly uncomfortable situations. Applying non-judgemental awareness has to become a familiar habit, and one that we build on gradually.

Intense emotions and tangled feelings

Sometimes, during an intense emotional situation, when you turn your attention inside, you find a jumble of chaotic emotions, some perhaps conflicting with others, some perhaps quite painful. You might feel overwhelmed by certain feelings and thoughts that seem to fuel each other in a kind of vicious circle. Such a state feels horrible and confusing, to the point that it can seem almost impossible to see through the tangle. In such a state of emotional dysregulation, it's easy to see how we might lash out or otherwise react in ways we'd rather not.

Bringing mindful attention to this tangle means noticing and allowing the whole crazy mess of feelings to be there without considering that any of them are right or wrong, or something you should or shouldn't have. Doing this in the heat of the moment isn't easy. It takes strength and a great deal of kindness. Know that you don't need to do anything about the tangle of feelings right now. Notice what the chaotic jumble feels like in your body and let it have its space (as much as you can in that moment).

Sometimes strong feelings can blind us to other, more subtle sensations and signals. It's like eating a curry that's so spicy you can't taste anything else, or trying to hear the clock ticking when there's music blaring out of the stereo. The quieter sensation might be trying to tell us something important but is drowned out.

Let's look at an example to help explain what this means. You're at a party and you get chatting to someone you haven't met before. The conversation is good, but every time they laugh it sets your teeth on edge. It's not long before you make your excuses and move away. Later, you feel bad for leaving them because they were nice. If we now look at this example from the perspective of someone who's got an established habit of awareness, we can see what happened. You're enjoying the conversation, but every time they laugh you notice a tightening in your belly that makes you feel slightly sick and a clenching in your jaw. You notice a compulsion to leave the room. Instead, you ask yourself what you're feeling beyond the obvious. What are the quieter, more subtle sensations and feelings? You begin to realize that their facial expression when they laugh reminds you of an ex from a few years ago with whom you had a difficult breakup. The (initially subconscious) memory was kicking up strong feelings that were overpowering the more gentle feelings centred on the social interaction and conversation. With that realization, you find their laugh stops affecting you so strongly and you can fully engage in the conversation.

Sometimes, especially when you're just starting out with a mindful approach, it might be much later when you realize there were more subtle feelings present underneath the strong ones. I remember a few years ago when I was doing psychotherapy, my therapist would ask me how I felt when my mum neglected to ask me how I was during our weekly phone call. I always wanted her to ask and felt frustrated when she didn't – but found it difficult to describe what I felt beyond that. The more I practised tuning in to my body, the sooner after the call I'd notice that I'd become frustrated and could ask myself what else I was feeling. I felt uncared for, and with that came a tightening in my chest and a longing that things were different. Gradually, I was able to notice nearer and nearer the time, until I was able to sense a whole variety of underlying feelings and storylines arising actually during the phone call. I was then able to describe this to my mum and that gave us an opportunity to start talking about what was happening between us.

Unwillingness to acknowledge what you're feeling

When continuing to look within with honesty and acceptance, you might uncover a sense of resistance or unwillingness to face just how you're feeling. Perhaps it feels like acknowledging whatever it is might overwhelm you or be like opening some kind of Pandora's Box.

Let's look at another example: Oscar regularly sees his mum. Despite the fact that he's a grown adult, whenever he spends time with her, she still nags him like he is a child. She tells him to stand up straight, stop wasting his money on expensive holidays and asks with monotonous regularity when he's going to find someone and settle down. Not realizing that the effect of all these little comments is cumulative, he finds himself getting angry after each remark – way above what he deems reasonable for such a throwaway comment. But in thinking that he shouldn't be getting so angry, he's unwilling to accept the full extent of his feelings, and, in effect, he's suppressing them.

Here's a different example: Kate has a strained and uncomfortable relationship with a female colleague at work. On the one hand she knows she wants to get to know her colleague more, but on the other feels an enormous resistance to letting herself do that. Secretly she knows she's attracted to her. Kate can't admit to herself that she might be gay and feels ashamed of her feelings, and is therefore unwilling to fully acknowledge what's actually going on.

In these situations, the first mindful step is to do your best to be open to whatever feelings are arising, however unexpected, unwanted or painful. It doesn't matter whether you think you should or shouldn't be feeling like this. It doesn't matter whether you like your feelings or not – or think they're crazy, out of proportion or a good/bad thing. That's what you feel. However hard you try, you can't change in this moment. Being willing to face the whole of what you're feeling takes great courage – together with great kindness and honesty. I don't want to underplay how difficult this is and how much strength it takes to fully acknowledge how you're feeling. If you recognize yourself here, go gently. This work is about kindness as much as anything else.

If you do identify any previously unacknowledged emotions, it's important you let them arise fully and find a way to express them safely. To help with this step, in Zen we study koans, which is a Japanese word that literally means "case" or "precedent". Koans are often seemingly nonsensical phrases, stories or examples of situations that have led to someone's awakening in the past that we can study today. Their outwardly confusing or illogical appearance is designed to help jar us out of our habitual ways of perceiving the world and nudge us toward shifting our perspective on things.

A koan taken from the writings of the Chinese philosopher Confucius says: "A virtuous person is never alone."[7] In this phrase, Confucius is using the emotion of loneliness as an example. He's saying to you, as a virtuous person, that if you ever feel lonely you should do your best not to hold back or resist in any way; that you should let yourself completely become that feeling of loneliness. As that loneliness finds its expression within you – perhaps through a sob or a deep slump into a chair – you and the feeling of being alone blend into one. At that point there's no "you" feeling "lonely" – there's just loneliness. It may not feel comfortable, but that is how you are in that moment. As you and the feeling become one, you and the universe become one, and if you're one with the universe, with everyone in the entire world and every other world across the whole cosmos how can you be lonely? Thus, as Confucius says, a virtuous person is never alone. We can apply this same teaching to any emotion. When we let that emotion in, completely acknowledge it, accept it and express it, we *become* it 100 per cent. At that point we are no longer separate from the universe – we *are* the whole universe expressing itself in that moment.

There are two caveats to this teaching that it is important to be aware of.

First, it's vital that we find a way to safely express whatever emotion is arising. People who formally become Buddhists take on the precepts (a set of guidelines that describe a wholesome life, including the precepts not to kill, steal, lie and so on). These can serve as a safety barrier around how we express strong emotions to make sure we do no harm. But we don't need to take the precepts in order to set that intention. We can just aim to do no harm in any of this work.

Second, it's important that we do our best not to become attached to the emotion as we explore letting it in fully. The emotion is merely a visitor in the abode of our being. It, like everything else, will arise and pass. Holding onto it or harbouring it in any way won't serve us or anyone around us. This is not about learning to tolerate difficult emotions or becoming a door mat for inappropriate or abusive behaviour. This is about learning to acknowledge our emotions as fully as we can – we let them arise and be expressed as appropriately and as much as possible (while doing our best not to do any harm), letting them fade or dissolve when they're ready, without holding on as they do so.

Restoring emotional regulation

As we've mentioned already, when we notice we're becoming dysregulated in the face of a troublesome person, the critical first step is becoming aware of what we're feeling – noticing, for example, the rising energy, the tension or the impulse to act or speak – and acknowledging it as fully as we can with an attitude of openness. Staying regulated as things get heated or emotionally charged isn't easy. It's something that we need to practise and build up to. It's hard to find a way to let the initial upsurge of emotions settle even a little before reacting to it. And even harder still is actually remembering to turn your attention inward when in the middle of a troublesome interaction. So how do we return to that balanced, aware, regulated state? There are actually two ways: by yourself or with the help of others.

In certain situations we may feel the need to move out of the turbulent rapids – to step away from people, get some distance and go somewhere quiet. In that quiet we might find we're able to settle and reflect on what's going on. One of the effects of the fight or flight reaction is that the attention gets narrowed. Our brain becomes focused on survival, and as a result our ability to think laterally and creatively diminishes. So if you can find a quiet place, try to mentally zoom out of the situation and tune into what's going on in your body. A relaxed, calm mind is better at seeing the wider perspective. To aid this process of regulation, doing something soothing for yourself can be helpful – like sitting with a nice hot drink or having a bath (of course we need to be careful we're not just distracting ourselves).

In different situations we may be able to regulate ourselves better with the help of others. We might start to feel dysregulated when interacting with a troublesome person while in the company of other trusted or safe people. If those other people are more regulated than us, then looking toward them can quickly help us calm down from our heightened emotional state. Humans, like other mammals, are more socially attuned. One person's emotional state can "magnetize" others to that level via what is known as our "social engagement system".[8] For example, imagine sitting in the office conference room alongside your colleagues, waiting for your boss to arrive to give his or her presentation. When the boss walks into the room, they're visibly tense, moving jerkily and obviously stressed out. In just a few minutes, everyone in the room also starts to feel agitated and tense as they resonate with the boss' dysregulated state. What's important here, though, is that the same thing can happen in reverse. Let's turn the example around – you're the boss arriving at the conference room to give your presentation after just having to discipline and almost fire one of your senior managers for his behaviour. You feel tense and scattered. You look around the room and fortunately make eye contact with someone in the second row that's sitting calmly with a kind and gentle expression on their face. That moment of connection with someone who is solidly regulated helps you calm down and re-establish a modicum of your own stability.

All young children have only the second method available to them – they rely on others to help them regulate. This is because both their threat-detection circuitry still hasn't fully developed and they haven't yet got to grips with how to modulate or temper their behaviour. A friend of mine who's a primary school teacher tells me she sees this all the time in her class. When there's a sudden loud noise or someone unexpected comes into the classroom, the children's ears prick up and they quickly turn to look at her. If they can't see her, they might start to get upset, but if they turn and find a calm face and neutral body posture, then they know there's no danger and feel reassured.

Helping friends to regulate

Learning about ourselves and our own reaction to troublesome people gives us a number of helpful tools that can be useful when we find ourselves around others who are struggling with troublesome people. As a friend (perhaps one of those trusted or safe people that we mentioned above), one of the best things you can do for someone who is becoming dysregulated in a troublesome encounter is to stay solidly regulated yourself. However, as we've mentioned, emotional states are highly contagious – we attune (magnetize) to others very easily. Some of the best yoga classes I've been to have started with the teacher quite obviously settled and regulated. I might have arrived having just been on the train, at work or in the shops and feeling quite unsettled. I'd be aware of my mind critically chewing over the day's events or worrying about to-do lists. But when I saw and felt the teacher in a state of regulation, looking, acting and exuding calm and steadiness, my body couldn't help but resonate with that and start to settle too.

When we're around someone who's dysregulated (for example, having a panic attack), it's hard to remain settled and steady yourself. That's why it's helpful to know a few tips. The first and most important thing is to make sure you develop a habit of mindfulness. Having that sensitivity and awareness as a matter of course puts you in a much better place to notice the early warning signs of being pulled out of your regulated state. You can then adjust your behaviour much more quickly. Our social engagement system is designed to be sensitive to facial expressions, voice tone and body posture. So try to make yourself appear as unthreatening (safe) as possible in order to soothe their threat-detection circuits. You can soften your facial expression (consciously relax your forehead and jaw), reassure them with a calm and neutral tone with naturally varied intonation (your normal tonal ups and downs) and use simple, short sentences. Adopt a relaxed posture (for example, uncross your arms and legs and loosen your hands) and model a steady, natural breathing pattern. You could call this purposefully misattuning yourself to the person you're interacting with in order to help them settle and steady. As they see you visibly settling yourself, they'll magnetize to you, rather than the other way around. Much of this is now taught on the standardized Mental Health First Aid course all around the world because it's effective in a range of situations where people might flip their lid and lose self-control.

Lastly, it's important to acknowledge that maintaining emotional regulation takes mental resources. Staying aware takes concentration, a certain level of vigilance to filter out our judgements and criticisms and a strong intention to be kind in the face of irritation or thoughtlessness. This means that maintaining emotional regulation becomes especially difficult when there are other demands on your system like work stresses or time pressures. For example, a friend of mine recently told me how she finds it difficult to cope with talking to her rather pedantic and old-fashioned dad in the evening after work because her mind is still caught up with the demands of the day. She finds it much easier at the weekend when she's more relaxed. Thus in times of added stress, it's important you cut yourself some extra slack and do your best to avoid particularly troublesome situations if possible.

CHAPTER 3
PATTERNS AND TENDENCIES – COPING STRATEGIES

So far we've looked at some ways in which troublesome interactions can show us why we become temporarily emotionally dysregulated (and hence are much more likely to lash out or do something we later regret). Now let's explore what our troublesome encounters can teach us about our more general patterns, habits and attitudes.

Attachment theory

Developed over the past 60 years or so, attachment theory[9] provides a helpful context through which we can understand how some of our emotional and interpersonal behavioural patterns become established. In essence, the theory describes the types of psychological bonds we're able to make with others as a consequence of the type and quality of relationships we had as infants with our primary caregivers (such as our parents). It proposes that an infant creates a "secure attachment pattern" when their caregivers were available and responsive to their needs and sufficiently reliable in that offering. This secure base creates a foundation for the child to explore the world, knowing that there's always a safe and nurturing place to return to. The theory proposes that things take a different turn when a caregiver is less nurturing or dependable.

For example, if an infant learns that in order to get their needs met and receive sufficient, safe nurturing, they mustn't demand too much from their caregiver (perhaps the caregiver was often preoccupied or otherwise absent) or they will have their requests for closeness repeatedly rejected, then they may either learn to withdraw (this is what's known in the theory as a "dismissive/avoidant attachment pattern"), or do the complete opposite: become especially demanding (creating an "anxious attachment pattern"). As they grow up, children living in this pattern subconsciously come to believe their needs essentially won't be met. Children who learn to withdraw might, as adults, have difficulty in trusting others, including authority figures. They may deny the importance of loved ones and see themselves as independent. Children in the anxious pattern might, as adults, hold on to their loved ones for dear life and, as a result, may be drawn to authority figures.

Alternatively, if a child's caregiver was sometimes loving and present and sometimes absent – or even frightening or abusive – the child might end up in an "ambivalent" or "disorganised" attachment pattern. The child may conclude that the times the caregiver was absent or frightening were their fault. As an adult they may constantly doubt themselves and their relationships. They may crave security and intimacy but feel fearful that the people they get close to will leave them, or go to great lengths to receive attention and affection but refuse to reciprocate this. At the extreme end, they may end up chaotic and explosive. It's a sad fact that adults can also be drawn into relationships that are destructive or hurtful simply because the attachment style feels familiar to their experiences in childhood – and hence predictable. In this situation, supportive relationships with healthy boundaries may feel abnormal and unpredictable, even though they may actually offer more nurture and safety for everyone involved.

Attachment theory gives one way of understanding *how* children end up adopting certain behavioural patterns as a result of the quality of their nurture. However, in mindfulness we're not really concerned with the whys and wherefores of how things came about. Mindfulness is about seeing things as they are in this moment and accepting that truth. Furthermore, the defensive strategies a child might instinctively adopt don't always have an easy correspondence with the patterns that propagate into adulthood.[10] Thus I'd like to look at adult behavioural patterns from a slightly different angle and through a Buddhist lens.

However we ended up with them, as adults we all have a preferred or default behavioural style when it comes to coping with difficult people or situations. That's not to say we always behave in that way, but it's just a characteristic habit. I'm going to categorize these styles into three camps: "the forces of pull", "the forces of push" and "the forces of delusion/ignorance". People in the "pull" camp habitually behave in a desiring, wanting or needy way around troublesome people. People in the "push" camp typically behave by either getting angered or avoiding the situation (both are forms of aversion, pushing feelings or people away). People in the "delusion" camp operate from misperceptions or misunderstandings that they think are real. According to the Buddha, aversion, craving and delusion are the three underlying causes of suffering. Let's explore these push-pull and delusion patterns in more detail.

Craving-desire pattern

Some people with this pattern crave attention. As a result, they might put up with absolutely terrible treatment just to get it

– feeling that any attention is better than nothing. Others want people to like them and may also blame themselves for what is going wrong in a relationship. If someone is grating on them, they might take swift action to appease the other person in order to soften the difficulty and prevent them from thinking ill of them in any way. For example, Zeyn works in a team where one person is arrogant, self-centred and consistently belittles and ignores him. But instead of telling them how he feels, Zeyn frequently apologizes for his perceived inadequacies, promises that he'll work harder, thinks he should be more accepting of the other person's interaction style and even stands up for them in conversations with other colleagues.

Another craving-desire tendency is to overcompensate for any perceived shortcoming in a troublesome situation by being overly chatty or bubbly. I remember a friend once brought her new boyfriend to a weekend BBQ to meet our circle of friends. From the word go, the new boyfriend was over-the-top friendly. Now that I know him better, I can see that he had dialled up his laddish behaviour for the occasion and was cracking a lot of jokes and play-teasing everyone in an effort to be liked. In a social situation (including romantic ones) where one partner is more distant or closed off, a typical craving response would be feeling the need to draw the more closed partner "out of themselves".

Although being stuck in this craving pattern leads to a cycle of suffering that's difficult to break out of, aspects of this habit can be useful at certain times. For example, that desire can motivate you to stick with or persevere in a relationship where others might quit prematurely.

If you recognize this pattern in yourself, you can begin working to soften this habit by looking with honesty at what it is you're craving. In Zen, we explore this through the koan "Seizei is destitute". The story goes that the monk Seizei once came to his teacher, Sozan (who lived 840–901 in China), and said, "Seizei is utterly destitute. Will you give him support?" Sozan called out, "Seizei!" Seizei replied, "Yes, sir!" Sozan said,

"You have finished three cups of the finest wine in China and still you say you have not yet moistened your lips!"

With his opening statement, Seizei is claiming complete poverty and he's asking his teacher to help him out. He's in the mindset of thinking that what he needs is outside of himself and (in this case) something his teacher can give him. (In truth, Seizei may have been a monk of some understanding and his opening request could be seen as a feint to test his teacher.) In response, Sozan calls out his name and Seizei replies, "Yes, sir!" With this call and response, Sozan is taking Seizei by the hand and leading him to the place of oneness, of immediacy, of intimacy with things-as-they-are. By getting him to answer directly, without thought, Sozan is showing him the true land of plenty where we lack for absolutely nothing because actually we *are* the whole universe. With deep kindness, he finally spells this out for Seizei by pointing out that he's already been drinking the finest wine in China, and "still you say you have not yet moistened your lips" – you say you're destitute, yet here you are with it all, right here!

Sometimes, like Seizei, it's difficult for us to see that we actually lack nothing, right here and now. Are you destitute? What do you lack? (This important question is a part of a koan that was excerpted from the records of master Rinzai, the *Rinzairoku*: "Followers of the Way, as I see it, you are not different from Shakya [the Buddha]. Today in your manifold activities, what is it that you lack?")

What do you crave? Try sitting down with a pen and paper and, as honestly as you can, write down what you crave in your life – from the littlest things to the biggest. Try not to edit or censor what comes up – just write down whatever arises. Your job is to enquire, acknowledge and accept whatever you notice and be kind and compassionate with yourself. Desires and habit patterns have power when they're unconscious, but when they're out in the open and acknowledged, then much of their power evaporates. How would it be to go around in life drinking the finest wine of the universe? What would this nectar taste like?

Aversion-anger pattern

Some people tend to react to troublesome people or situations by becoming frustrated and angry. It's important to realize that anger is an essential and useful emotion. It gives us the strength to take appropriate, assertive action when necessary to ensure the wellbeing or survival of ourselves and others. However, if left unattended, the anger can fester, creating inner turmoil, negative thoughts and physical tension. If it's left to grow beneath our awareness, it can easily intensify to explosion level where it's much harder to express safely. Thus we need to know how to manage it wisely. Dealing with frustration and anger can happen on three levels – depending on your ability to stay present with the sensations as they build and handle the concomitant emotional energy that's released into your system.

1 **Vent the anger safely.** Already this requires a level of self-awareness and control so that we can hold the build-up of energy until we're somewhere safe. Safe ways of venting might include punching a pillow, going for a run or shouting loudly in the middle of a field.
2 **Ground the energy.** This takes a little more practice and awareness of the energy around anger. To do this you can touch the ground and intend the anger to drain out of you. Like a lightning rod connected to the ground, touching the earth is like psychologically grounding yourself. You can imagine the hot, bright anger energy flowing out of your hand into the earth and being released.
3 **Redirect the energy.** This third level asks us to appreciate that the energy anger liberates within our system isn't inherently good or bad. Through our practice we can work to skilfully redirect or channel that energy into a kind of fierce compassion that motivates us to take positive action. I remember the Dalai Lama said once in a talk that we should always be thankful to people who make us angry – precisely because they liberate energy that we can use for good.

People who get angry around troublesome people may often end up in confrontations or fights (especially if the other person also angers easily). That leads us to the next Zen koan we are going to explore: "How do you stop a fight on the other side of the river?" This koan is designed to get us to look at conflict and how we deal with it from a Zen perspective.

However, before we go any further, let's briefly look at another koan to help us understand how to work with this type of question – the koan of master Joshu's *Mu*. The story goes that a monk approached Joshu (who lived in 9th-century China) and asked, "Does a dog have Buddha-nature?" Joshu answered: "*Mu!*" At first glance this seems to not make any sense (especially if you know that *mu* is a Japanese word, pronounced *wu* 無 in the original Chinese story, that means "no" or "not" and is most commonly used as a negative prefix, like "un-" in English). But as we explore *mu* more, we come to know the mind of Joshu in the moment he answered in that way.

When we start out, *mu* is a confusing concept that seems far away, foreign and impenetrable. As we learn to put aside our initial judgements about it not making any sense, the person looking at *mu* and *mu* itself can get closer and closer – until eventually they merge. This is the point where the camera lens through which we perceive the world shifts and we see things not from a perspective of separation but from one of non-separation or non-duality. We step into the mind of awakening by becoming *mu*, and by doing that, the apparent separation between us and the entire universe vanishes.

So how do you stop a fight on the other side of the river? At face value, if we're here and it's over there, how can we? This could equally be "How can you stop the fighting in some far-away war-torn country?" or "How can you stop a fight in the next room?" or indeed "How can you stop a fight when you're right in the middle of one and you're about to lash out?"

Things escalate into conflict when the psychological or emotional distance between the two parties becomes insurmountable. An enormous gulf opens up, big enough to hold a vast river, as the koan suggests. But this distance is there only when we perceive things through the lens of our conventional view in which everything is distinct, separate and self-contained. As with Joshu's *mu*, if we really begin looking at this question of how to stop a fight, then the question and the questioner (you) get closer and closer – like two wrestlers moving toward each other in the ring. Eventually – as happens when the two wrestlers wrap their arms and legs around each other – the fight over there, across the other side of the river, disappears from view. We find that there is no fight out there and no one who sees the fight. There is only fighting! At this point we literally become the fight. And when we do that, we step into the perspective of non-separation, of oneness. We see that this other person is as separate from us as our right hand is from our left. And when have you known one hand to fight with the other?

Granted, it's not easy to find this perspective in the heat of the moment. We have to build up the wherewithal through consistent practice to maintain our non-judgemental awareness of what's going on and how we feel – but it is possible.

The next koan we're going to look at brings our attention to arguments and disagreements – another related outcome of the aversion-anger pattern. This koan recalls a situation in the monastery of the great 8th-century Zen master Nansen (who was the teacher of Joshu). The account begins with the monks from one side of the monastery arguing with the monks from the other side of the monastery over a cat. The koan doesn't tell us specifically what they were arguing about, but just by getting involved in a petty argument the monks were failing to show any level of insight or compassion. It's at this point that Nansen walks in – and we can only imagine how he felt when he found his own monks arguing like this. So Nansen grabs the cat, pulls out a knife and says, "You monks! If you can say a word of Zen I will spare the cat. Otherwise, I will kill it." He was giving them all another chance to show him that they'd understood something of what he'd taught them. The account says no one could answer, so Nansen cut the cat in two.

At face value, this might seem like a cruel way to get his point across. He may very well have actually sliced the cat in half, but the story can also be viewed in a metaphorical or symbolic way. An argument starts because we have a conflicting viewpoint. I think "I'm right and you're wrong". This is about as dualistic and separate as it gets. Nansen was trying to get his monks to break out of this mindset and see the non-dual perspective where the concepts of right and wrong and of you and me dissolve. When we study the koan, this is what it's encouraging us to do.

In his response to this case, the 12th-century Japanese Zen master Dogen wrote that if he was one of the quarrelling monks, he might have said: "You know how to cut the cat in two with one sword, but you don't know how to cut the cat in one with one sword."[11] The killing of the cat allegorically represents cutting off the dualistic mind – the one where there are two halves of a cat, I feel separate from you and my view is more "right" – so we can step into the non-dual mind. The cat is cut into one. Yelp!

In the next scene of the koan, Nansen meets his senior student Joshu after he gets back from a shopping trip and relates what happened. In response, Joshu doesn't utter a word, but simply takes off his sandal, puts it on his head and walks out. Nansen responds admiringly, "If you had been there, the cat would have been saved!" Granted, Joshu's response seems bizarre. But what's important is that Joshu didn't get drawn into the argument over the cat, or say what should or shouldn't have been done. He simply expressed the essence of Zen – in his own idiosyncratic way – through a spontaneous, direct action that arose out of the mind of awakening. That was the type of response that Nansen was looking for in the quarrelling monks when he asked for "a word of Zen".

And, through this koan, that's what Nansen is looking for in us. In the middle of an argument, consider your viewpoint on the situation and your worldview. If we remain in the mindset of "I'm right and you're wrong", the conflict will inevitably continue. All that will happen is that each party will harden their position more and more until the problem becomes intractable. It's up to us to ask whether this is the only way of seeing things. Can we look at the situation from a different perspective? Can we see that we're in this together and that both of us are co-creating this suffering? Can the right hand stop arguing with the left?

Aversion-avoidance pattern

There are those who fall into the aversion pattern, but rather than getting angered by troublesome people or situations, they react by avoiding them. Let's look at a few examples.

- Henry finds someone in his common friendship group difficult, so always makes an excuse to avoid meeting up with the group if he knows they'll be there.
- On Ella's usual walking route to the shops, she always bumps into someone who corners her and complains about everything that's going on in their life. As a result, Ella has started to take a different route (even though it takes longer).
- Millie is a school teacher, and has started to notice that she often avoids phoning the more difficult parents about their child's behaviour because she finds it incredibly awkward. If she does find the courage to phone and has to leave a message, she then feels relieved when they don't call back. She's aware her avoidance means the issues aren't getting tackled properly, but still finds herself in this pattern again and again.

Unfortunately there are lots of ways we can avoid dealing with difficult people, making this one of the easiest patterns to fall into. However, because avoidance is something that often happens below the level of consciousness, it is also a difficult pattern to work with – if we're not aware of it, how do we know there's something we need to deal with? This is where friends or family can be helpful – other people will often spot you're avoiding something before you do, so listen carefully if they ever suggest you're in a pattern of avoidance.

Denial

Only in certain situations is it possible to totally avoid a troublesome person. We refer to these people as troublesome because they generate challenging and uncomfortable emotions within us. As humans, we're wired at the subconscious level to move toward pleasure and away from pain. Because we dislike uncomfortable feelings, our brain has many more tricks up its sleeve than just avoidance to move us away from that discomfort.

One simple thing the brain can do is deny the feelings even exist. Let's look at some straightforward examples to illustrate what this means.

- More and more evidence comes to light that Amy's partner is having an affair, but her mind simply won't admit it. Her unconscious mind thinks that accepting that reality will be too painful and will lead to confrontation and more pain, so acts to "protect" her by denying it.
- Brendon has been told by his doctor that he is morbidly obese, but continues to think that he's just "big-boned", so can't see why he would need to change his eating habits.
- Tiana lives in a house-share with four others, including someone she's known for years. This person has become difficult to live with and the others are requesting that, because she knows them the best, she asks them to move out. Each time Tiana reflects on how difficult the housemate is behaving, she just can't see what the problem is.

Back when I first began paying closer attention to my inner world, I noticed that in difficult situations I also adopted a denial approach: I would go numb. After my traumatic childhood experiences, my subconscious had learnt to block out vast swathes of my internal world from conscious awareness in order to avoid feeling pain. In my adolescent years I began gravitating toward the study of the emotionally undemanding subjects of mathematics and physics, meaning I could get away with continuing to exist in my rather impoverished world of sensations and feelings. But only up to a point. At 25, I'd never had a romantic relationship, and my relationships with my family were formal at best and, at times, hurtful. I remember things came to a head during one Easter holiday when I was back from university and my mum recommended that I find some help. As difficult as it was to hear, it was good advice! Through the reflective lens of psychotherapy, I learnt to see how my unconscious had adopted this denial technique as a way of avoiding the pain of separation and loss – first when my father was expelled after it was found out that he'd abused me, and later when my stepfather died and my mum was severely injured in the car accident. Over time, this response solidified into a habit, to the point where I avoided situations where people might get emotionally close to me and also numbed myself to any feelings of emotional connection that did arise.

Here's another slightly more complex example involving someone I'm going to call Maurice. A while ago, Maurice developed a crush on a colleague and started having regular sexual fantasies about her. He told himself these were totally inappropriate and tried hard to banish them from his mind. Now, a few years later, these fantasies still arise – but as they do, Maurice has learnt to push them away and convince himself that they never happened. Because his self-deception has become automatic, he now no longer has a conscious way of managing his sexual thoughts in regard to this colleague. Without this awareness, there's a likelihood that, one day, he might act impulsively and do something abusive. This is why it's absolutely critical that we acknowledge and accept our thoughts and feelings – however good, bad or ugly they are – as much as we can, with kindness and openness. Thoughts in themselves don't cause actions. Only when we know and fully accept our thoughts and feelings can we assess how best to respond to them appropriately.

Distraction

Another trick the unconscious mind can play is distraction. We know that strong sensations can overwhelm weaker ones. Distraction works by overwhelming a painful feeling with an equal or stronger pleasurable one. For example, I had a friend once who had regular line-management meetings at work with a boss she found arrogant and condescending. She dreaded these meetings and in the hour that preceded the appointment, she noticed she always ended up eating a whole slab of chocolate. The pleasurable taste (to some degree) acted to override or cover over the feelings of anxiety and trepidation. In another example, someone is having difficulties in their relationship, so spends all their spare time out playing golf instead of confronting the situation.

If you know you're an avoidant type, you can practise with this behavioural pattern by consciously moving toward some of the things that you're averse to. Start with something easy – like a chore. If you hate washing up and always find ways of avoiding doing it, then try noticing if this aversion has a physical trace in the body – perhaps a sense of tiredness or heaviness as you approach the sink. Try to really zoom in to the sensations without feeling like you need to judge them in any way. What is it specifically that you don't like? When you come to actually do the washing up, keep in contact with your feelings and watch as they change and shift. You may never come to like washing up, but you can learn to be okay with that feeling of dislike. If you can consciously work with your habitual avoidance of something as simple and non-threatening as the washing up, then gradually you can practise moving toward people and situations you would normally avoid. Just becoming aware that you are avoiding something is half the work done already. Once you're aware of the feeling, you can choose to respond to it wisely.

Aspects of the avoidance pattern can sometimes be helpful. It may be healthier to simply avoid certain difficult people in the short term if we're feeling particularly vulnerable or raw – for example after a relationship breakup or confrontation at work. But in the long term, if this ends up being our default method for dealing with troublesome people, then at best we're only postponing the difficulty, and at worst we're denying ourselves so much of life's potential.

Delusion pattern

In Buddhism, delusion is one of the primary causes of suffering. It means a kind of ignorance or deep-seated misperception of reality, or mistaking illusion to be reality. As an example of this pattern, we can imagine someone who is naturally gregarious and confident in their social interactions. When another person annoys them or if they annoy someone else, they just barrel through regardless with a general lack of awareness, quite blind to the consequences of their actions. If anyone confronts them about their behaviour they just ignore them or laugh it off.

Identifying that we're operating from a deluded viewpoint is tricky, because before we realize our viewpoint is deluded it feels totally real. It takes deep enquiry and honesty and an effort to truly listen to the views and comments from others who recognize what's going on. It might take years to see and accept you have been behaving in this pattern – or, as happened in the following example, it might be shattered in an instant.

A friend of mine recently told me about an evening with his wife, not long after they started living together, when she briefly turned into a troublesome person for him. She had just got back from a weekend away with some friends and they were sitting together chatting about how it had gone. On the Saturday night she'd been out to a dance club and described how sometime during the night she'd been offered some drugs and had accepted. At this revelation, my friend told me he got extremely angry and physically started to tremble. After the initial emotion had subsided, they were able to continue to talk about it. After a few weeks of reflection, he realized what had happened. He had fixed his wife into a "thing". He had created an idealized version of her – the way he thought she was, behaving in the way he had imagined her to – and was operating with the belief that that's who she was. So when she described an action that wasn't something his imagined fantasy of her would do, his delusion was shattered – and that's why he had become so upset. She wasn't who he thought she was – and indeed she isn't! His delusion was thinking he'd pinned her down – making her into an object in his mind – when in fact she's actually a dynamic, ever-changing, interconnected process that cannot be objectified. He told me he feels lucky that he recognized this early on in his relationship. For many people, this happens after they've been together for some years. With time, we develop the impression that we know everything about our partner. But how can we? Scientists still don't claim to understand everything about the simplest materials, so how can you ever know everything about another person?

In working in the area of delusions, it's important to keep at the back of your mind the idea that you could be wrong. As much as you can in everything you do, maintain an openness of mind and a willingness to test your assumptions and opinions. Even if you're convinced that something someone's asked you to do isn't going to work, give them the benefit of the doubt. You could be wrong. Another approach that's helpful is to take the long view. Try to identify any recurring patterns in your relationships. For example, you might realize that people always start avoiding you after a certain time of knowing you, or feel like you're always the one to end the relationship, or see that minor conflicts frequently escalate into big fights. These patterns may hint at certain hidden views or beliefs that are influencing your behaviour.

As with everything that we bring our mindful attention to, the object is not to judge or criticize. We do our best to simply acknowledge what we find with as much honesty and openness as we can. What we uncover may not be that easy or pleasant to accept. One of the common blocks to identifying delusions is that it might feel more comfortable to continue operating within that delusion than actually face up to the fact that you might be deluded.

Take it slowly and know that whatever views or beliefs you uncover almost certainly developed from you trying to do your best at the time.

CHAPTER 4
SOFTENING WITH COMPASSION

When we're faced with a troublesome person, our attitude can quickly become defensive. We stiffen up in an attempt to protect ourselves from any potential injury – whether that be to our physical body or to our fragile sense of self. We assert our moral correctness and apportion blame, thinking the situation is their fault; they're the ones needing to change and they're the ones causing me to feel this way. Very easily we stop actually listening, and let our preconceived assumptions and opinions take over.

All this cements our perceived distinction between "that difficult person" and "me". As we've said previously, at this point we are firmly standing on the ground of duality, of separation – and therefore of suffering. Even entertaining the possibility that you might play a part in creating these unpleasant feelings is uncomfortable.

But, if we can bring a sincere awareness and open-minded enquiry to what's going on, our initial hard stance will soften into something much broader and more inclusive. We start to see how our past experiences and past suffering have laid the foundations for the development of the habit patterns and worldviews that contribute to our reactions – just as much as they have for our troublesome person.

Habits and beliefs are fixed patterns of behaviour and thought. If we continue holding on to them after they've served their usefulness, they become restrictive and confining. They only serve to limit us. In order to live in the present moment with flexibility and adaptability, we need to learn when it's appropriate to let go. There's an old Zen parable that captures this very well.

A senior monk and a junior monk were travelling together. At one point, they came to a river with a strong current. As the monks were preparing to wade across, a young woman approached and asked if they could help her cross too. Without a thought, the senior monk picked up this woman, carried her on his shoulders across the river and put her down on the other side. The junior monk was upset but said nothing. A little while later, as they continued on their journey, the senior monk noticed that the junior monk was quiet and asked if something was the matter. The younger monk said: "As monks, we are not permitted to touch women. How could you carry that woman on your shoulders?" The older monk looked at him and replied: "Brother, I left her a long time ago at the bank of the river, however you seem to still be carrying her!"

The older monk was able to respond flexibly to the situation and remain in the present moment as he continued on the journey (whether or not he did the right thing is a matter of interpretation). However, the younger monk, bound by ideas, rules and what should or shouldn't be done, spent his time silently fuming in disbelief at what the senior monk had done – and as a result probably missed seeing the beautiful gardens next to the river.

As we begin seeing and acknowledging the way we are around troublesome people (and thus letting go of how we want or wish things to be), it's critical we're compassionate with ourselves. The word compassion comes from the Latin "com" meaning to be with and "passion", which is the old word for pain or suffering (as in "the passion of Christ"). Compassion therefore means to *be with* pain, difficulty and suffering. Letting go of things that no longer serve us is an act of compassion.

In Buddhism, compassion is said to be one of the two pillars of practice (the other being insight or wisdom). Not long after I first started studying Zen, I remember facing the koan: "How many directions does the eye of compassion look?" Zen isn't well known for emphasizing compassion, but that reflects a misconception about Zen. It's true, compassion isn't always spoken about as directly in Zen as it is in other schools of Buddhism, but that doesn't mean it's not equally there. The "eye of compassion" is an allusion to *Avalokiteshvara*, the embodiment of the Buddhist ideal of compassion. *Avalokiteshvara* is a Sanskrit name that means "hearer of the sounds/cries of the world". The Japanese translation is *Kannon* (or in Chinese, *Guanyin*). In Japan, *Kannon* is often portrayed in feminine form with eleven heads to see and hear all the suffering in the world. But there's more to the embodiment of compassion than just listening; there's a connotation of a wish to alleviate that suffering. So *Kannon* is also depicted as having 1,000 arms to let her reach out and help all those in need.

So how many directions do the eyes and ears of Kannon look? Every direction, it seems. I remember presenting this answer to my teacher. In response he said: "Show me." I pointed all around the room, including up and down. "Good", he said, "but not quite." I sat considering this for a while, trying to think what other direction there is. Those in the caring professions often suffer from this blindness too. Many pour out compassion to their patients and clients, then some way down the line find themselves burnt out. Feeling knackered and poorly in bed, all they can think of is the people they're letting down and when they can get back out there. So what's the extra direction? Finally I twigged – I pointed toward myself and my teacher smiled. It's essential that our eye of compassion not only looks outwards in every direction, but also inward. How can we truly be of help in the world if we don't look after ourselves and our own health and wellbeing?

As we allow troublesome people to become our teachers, they start to show us more and more where we're blocked, where we're holding on and where we're avoiding the truth. If we can see the things they teach us with an attitude of non-judgement, self-compassion and maybe even humour, then that'll put us in the best possible position to let go and respond as wisely as we can in any given situation.

In Part 2, we're going to look in more detail at some of the main arenas of life where troublesome people crop up, including in everyday life, in the workplace and at home. In each arena we'll explore a selection of true stories of how people have responded to their troublesome person and found deep learning from their encounter. These stories originate from a diverse range of people from the Zen community I'm part of (including myself), mostly in the UK but also abroad. I've changed the names and altered some details to preserve the anonymity of those that I have interviewed. Hearing from others can help us see what's possible, and that truly amazing things can happen when we honestly face what's actually happening. It's my hope that you can see aspects of yourself and your own situation in one or two of these examples.

PART TWO
TROUBLESOME ARENAS

CHAPTER 5
FELLOW-TRAVELLER BUDDHAS

Encounters with troublesome fellow travellers are, most often, one-off incidents with people you've never met before and will never meet again. Sometimes the troublesome Buddha isn't embodied in one individual but in a "type" of person or group of people, say, for example, those that start getting on the train before they let people off. Perhaps the behaviour you find troublesome happens again and again with different perpetrators (such as drivers who turn off without indicating). Given just a few minutes, we could all probably come up with a long list of behaviours we find infuriating in fellow travellers!

When we encounter a troublesome person, we easily jump into blaming them for the difficulty they're causing us. We think they're either acting on purpose – to spite us or as a personal insult (and, as a result, we take it personally) – or they're being selfish and they should know better. Either way, we assume they're, at some level, in control – or at least consciously aware of what they're doing.

The ancient Chinese Daoist philosopher Zhuangzi (Chuang Tzu) proposed in the 4th century BCE a perspective that is particularly helpful when thinking about difficult fellow travellers. Zhuangzi said if an empty boat collides with you on a river, then you're not going to be angry at the boat. But if a boat with a person in it is on a collision course, then you'll shout at the person to steer clear. If they don't appear to hear, you'll shout louder and start cursing, all because there is a person in the boat. If it were an empty boat, you wouldn't be getting angry.[12]

With this story, Zhuangzi is encouraging us to try and see our troublesome people like that empty boat. An empty boat doesn't collide with us on purpose; the encounter is due to a chance combination of occurrences and past conditions. Similarly, people aren't necessarily being purposefully difficult just to annoy you, so there is room to reframe your troublesome person's actions as compulsive, without specific purpose, and being driven by unconscious forces as a result of unexamined wounds and past experiences. They're just trying to do their best (given their circumstances) – or at worst, they're simply unaware of the potential effects of their behaviour. How might your reactions change when you perceive difficult behaviour through this kind of lens?

The following examples describe encounters with a variety of troublesome fellow travellers in some common situations and how they highlighted in each person certain stuck attitudes or preconceptions. The first is set on a busy staircase, the second two are on the train and the fourth in the car.

Imagining everybody as fragile vases

Not long ago, Gloria was walking down a packed shopping street in London, feeling irritable. She perceived everyone as "behaving like assholes, hungry for the shops", and realized that she was elbowing her way through the crowd as she tried to make headway. On a narrow staircase down into the underground station, she rushed past a women, forcing her to the side. The offended lady shouted back ironically: "I'm going down the stairs too you know!"

Gloria remembers that "at that moment, through those words, this obstacle in my way became a person". However, as quick as a flash, that person became "a bitch that wasn't going anywhere anyway, so deserved to be pushed out of the way". Gloria did her best to laugh at herself as she noticed these unkind, reactive and judgemental thoughts. She let the woman go ahead of her. In the next few moments, these thoughts gave way to a visceral realization that she herself was the one being an asshole and that "everyone around her was a person with their own feelings and goals". They weren't all personally trying to get in her way. She says: "It's so easy to forget this!"

After this encounter, she started to walk along "imagining everybody as fragile vases that could easily be broken or damaged". As soon as she did this, it brought up a deep sense of kindness and patience: "It's okay to take longer, if we respect everyone as people, not just obstacles in each other's way." Reflecting now, she says: "You think you don't have the energy to be nice, but this isn't true. You always have the energy." In practising being nice while on the pavement, Gloria has found a new sense of respect for her fellow pedestrians and a deep sense of shared humanity. She added: "This has been another reminder to me that we're all in this world together."

My own experience of listening to noises on a train

Increasingly, those of us trying to cultivate our skills in mindfulness use periods of our travel time, particularly the commute to work, to meditate. I've often spotted likely candidates on the train or bus: headphones in, sitting up straight with a clear intent, eyes closed for a few minutes at a time. When we try to meditate in less-than-ideal circumstances such as these, sounds can quickly become troublesome.

I remember sitting on a train once doing some meditation (without headphones), focusing on my breath, when someone a few rows ahead started to play a game on their phone – with the volume turned up. The same beeps and sound effects repeated again and again and I noticed myself gradually getting irritated. I thought: "Don't they know their volume is on? Can't they appreciate how annoying that is to everyone else?" After acknowledging these initial reactive thoughts, I realized that it wasn't the sound itself that was the problem; it was my resistance to it. My discomfort wasn't arising from the beeping, but from the difference between reality and what I wanted reality to be (quiet). As I acknowledged my frustration and irritation, and allowed those feelings to be there, they began to lose their intensity.

Before this incident happened, I'd read an article or two and listened to a few talks about how to deal with distractions in meditation. Remembering their recommendations, I tried my best to put aside the thoughts about who was to blame or how long the noise might go on for. I began opening my attention to the sounds – in fact to the whole soundscape around me in the train. Like that, I found a gentle acceptance for all the sounds: the beeping effects from that person's phone, the clackety-clack of the train wheels, the occasional slamming of the toilet cubicle door, the subtle squeaking of the bulkheads and the sound of people nattering behind me. I was enthralled by the huge variety of sounds and noises coming from all directions.

The sounds were no longer something separate from me that was interfering with my practice and making me irritated, but had become a part of my practice. More than that, I'd become part of the moment. As I realized that, I mentally thanked the person a few rows ahead of me, still obliviously playing away on their phone.

Becoming one with her commute and flowing

Patricia used to have a long commute to work in central London, taking at least one hour and forty minutes on the train and underground. She found the section on the underground the most difficult as the carriages at that time would always be overcrowded. She would sometimes have to wait for five or six trains before there was space for her to get on, and then she would be pushed and shoved. She remembers some people that she ended up being squeezed up against "were very strange". "The air was often hot and dirty," she recalled, "and sometimes there would be a lot of standing on the platform and the trains, making the journey quite physically demanding. Often the train would get held at a red signal for a long time and the experience was frequently not very pleasant."

For Patricia, this became an ideal time to put her Zen meditation into practice. She says: "I would try to be with each situation, and to *nari kiru* each moment" (*nari kiru* is a Japanese phrase used by our Zen teacher meaning "become one with"). Over time, Patricia says, "I started to experience the whole of my commute as a flow – waiting, getting on and off the trains, being pushed around, being one of a huge crowd." She realized that she'd stopped expecting anything. In these times, she felt like she would become "transparent and empty". Even though the experience was no less pleasant, she recognized that, as a result, she had stopped suffering. She remembers how this commute taught her a great deal about how to apply her Zen practice in daily life.

Thanking bad drivers for pointing out one's own grasping

Bill has always tried to be a courteous driver, but in the past few years he has noticed that one particular situation on the road has really got his back up: when the outside lane closes or ends on a multi-lane road while the traffic is heavy. "Particularly, it's those drivers who are desperate to get past you before the lane closes that really irritate me" – the ones that stay in the closing lane "trying to get just one more car in front and then having to brake hard and cut in at the last second". Surely, he thought, it was dangerous driving and it held him back in his own progress.

For a long time he thought this behaviour was "unjust". He remembers he saw it as "heroic when a larger vehicle would move out to straddle the outside two lanes in an attempt to stop these idiots from getting past and jumping the queue". He realized, "I actually didn't want these drivers to be in front of me, or to beat me" in the queue.

Then Bill saw a documentary about traffic flow on busy roads. It quoted research showing that vehicles that straddle two lanes cause more problems. It said that the optimal use of the road for heavy traffic flow is to use both lanes for as long as possible. Bill was fascinated how this new information totally changed his view. He started to see "those people who straddle or block lanes as idiots", thinking, "don't they know what they're doing?!"

Cognitively he knew that the safest and best thing is to let those people who want to get ahead just go past. "As long as they're not being unsafe, whatever they do makes no actual difference to me, and I don't need to worry why they're doing it." However, although he knew that it was technically better for traffic flow, he still observed a semi-conscious and immediate urge not to let them past. "I noticed a strong desire to speed up and close the gap so there would be no space for them to merge" – to essentially punish them for their behaviour. He questioned himself: "Why does some part of me want to do this when it's not actually something I consciously want to do?"

He saw this arising out of the "karmic seeds of thinking the thought so many times, creating a habitual, instant reaction". He surmised: "The impulse arises immediately, and only afterwards comes the cognitive thought of wanting to do the opposite." He added: "Now it makes me laugh how easily and quickly I beat myself up over this!"

After spending time observing and investigating these thoughts and habitual reactions, Bill has become grateful for these situations. "If it wasn't for those people cutting in, how would I have seen this grasping nature of mine? Grasping onto my position in the queue, and not wanting to be held back by these people."

Reflecting now, Bill says: "When I'm in this situation on the road, my habitual impulse is still there, but it's mellowed slightly. When it arises, I can see it more quickly, and I can pop it like a bubble." He chooses to let the car pass (or let it merge in front of him) and then: "I thank them out loud for showing me my attachments." Though he does admit: "I notice how good I feel for doing that, and the hint of smugness that comes with it – which I try to accept and not beat myself up for yet again!"

He finds it incredible just how much his perception and attitudes on the road have changed through his careful observation and enquiry, and he smiles regularly at these new discoveries and realizations in similar situations.

CHAPTER 6
WORKPLACE BUDDHAS

Most of us spend much of our waking life at work. Whether we spend that time in an office, on a farm, in a factory or online, we are required to develop "professional" relationships with people that we may not have chosen to spend so much time with otherwise. If we add to this the various financial strains, inequalities and power dynamics that play out up, down and across the lines of seniority, the workplace can quickly turn into a viper pit of troublesome people.

Traditionally, Buddhism divides existence into six different realms. There are the two we ordinarily know, the human and animal realms. Then there's the godly realm (inhabited by beings experiencing only pleasure and bliss), the realm of the hungry ghosts (populated by beings who are stuck in states of want, addiction and lack), the *asura* realm (consisting of beings who are driven by anger, jealousy and conflict; an *asura* is a kind of wrathful demi-god in the Buddhist cosmology) and the hell realm (consisting of various forms of intense suffering).

In Zen, these realms are seen as representing different states of existence that we can find ourselves in during our life. And in terms of our subject here, many workplaces could be seen as *asura* realms – full of people driven by anger, jealousy and ambition, where conflict, emotional violence, competition and backstabbing take centre stage, sociopathic bosses rule the roost and people do inexcusable things just to get a step ahead. This battle-for-survival mentality puts the body into a persistent state of emergency, and as the stress and anxiety rise, it becomes ever more difficult to be perceptive and empathetic to others. Unfortunately this angry, competitive, anxiety-filled state has become the norm in large swathes of society and its workplaces.

Of course not every workplace is like this, or like this all the time – as we'll see in the examples below. But even in the friendliest workplaces there might be times when the *asura* mentality arises. So what better place to apply awareness, compassion and honesty, and find out what we can learn from our troublesome colleagues and clients and the effect they have on us? In the following, we'll encounter examples of difficult people in a variety of workplaces, from the typical *asura* realm as described above, to much more supportive and caring environments.

Perception and reality are not the same thing

Pierre has had a colleague that he has struggled with for many years, perceiving her as "lazy and bad at her job". Every time she asked him to do something, he said he would "see her request as a further sign of her laziness". He remembers he "found it difficult not to react negatively and ended up feeling frustrated, annoyed, angry and tense". "All sorts of storylines about my colleague's apathy and lack of hard work would whirr around in my mind." He remembers that his habit of ruminating on these things just compounded the stress he was feeling.

During this time Pierre started learning mindfulness and practising meditation, and through this started to get to know his mind. "Over time I began to see more and more clearly how my agitated mental state over my colleague's perceived behaviour and the actual situation were two completely different things." He remembers: "All the ideas about how lazy my colleague was kept on circulating in my mind, but I gradually learnt how to feel at ease with them – knowing they were just thoughts." He began to recognize his preconceptions, fixed views and opinions as types of delusions, and cultivated a sense of compassion toward himself for having them. Pierre can now observe his desire to want things to go "his way", acknowledge that desire and just carry on with the task at hand. He says: "I now try to deal with each given situation and interaction with fresh eyes, doing my best not to bring my assumptions and preconceptions with me." He finds he's more able to let go of the thoughts about a situation once it has been dealt with.

Recently, Pierre has noticed an arising of gratitude toward his colleague. He admits his interactions with her have shone a light on his own delusions, his conditioned mental patterns and habits, where he was trying to hold on and where he was stuck, and his sense of separation from her and the world. In fact, he says: "She continues to be a great teacher to me." He's found that "each new encounter is a reminder of where I'm still holding on and where I can still grow and develop".

Pierre's example encapsulates an important insight – perhaps the most important of all when it comes to learning how to deal with difficult work colleagues and troublesome people in general: that perception and reality are two different things. This realization allowed Pierre to stop identifying with his thoughts and see them as types of delusions, which, in turn, allowed him to let go and stay more present in his interactions with his colleague and see her in a different light. But just because we've seen the difference once, or understand it intellectually, doesn't mean we will never again get trapped in perceptions and ideas. Noticing when we get caught in our preconceptions is a practice. This is why tuning in to certain bodily sensations (like discomfort or heat) can be vitally important, since they're often sensitive indicators that something is going on. We'll see this clearly in the following example.

The resistance to being fully present every time

Nadia works in a home as a carer for adults with learning difficulties. These people have become her troublesome Buddhas. She describes being around them: "Everything is magnified, including emotions, physical actions and demands. Not all of them have functioning social filters and many of them ask the same question over and over, day after day." For a long time Nadia questioned what the right response to these repeated questions might be. When she was new, she tried answering them every time, but she quickly got tired and bored of repeating the same answer.

Nadia has an established meditation practice and was used to checking in regularly with her bodily sensations. Answering the same question again and again, she said, "would cause an upwelling of tiredness and exhaustion that I felt as a discomfort in my body". She realized her mind's unconscious wish to avoid the discomfort led to her giving less and less attention to that interaction. She remembers finding herself "fading out what they were saying and trying to avoid eye contact in an attempt to discourage them from asking yet again". However, she said: "I knew in my heart this was the wrong approach." She realized her lack of attention would often cause her questioner to get agitated and ask even more determinedly. The physical sensations generated by frustration and fatigue became a sensitive indicator.

Although intellectually Nadia has known for a long time how important it is to be fully aware and present as you respond, each interaction with one of the home's residents became a physical, visceral reminder of this. "The more closely I tuned into my body, the more I could notice when I was subtly trying to avoid or push them away. The repeated questions became opportunities for me to fine-tune my ability to stay present." She would listen for the early warning signs of discomfort in herself and the questioner, signalling that she was slipping back into her habit of tuning out. "Straight away," she said, "I could see how my complete presence and attention improved the relationship and there would be fewer questions and less repetition."

"I can see how such a little change in my attitude has paid back a hundred times", she said. "For example, one chap who had always been difficult started attending the loving kindness meditation sessions that I ran in the home. Initially he was negative, but with time he really took it in and now often stops me and smiles, telling me with delight that he's done the meditation." Another woman that she had previously often faded out recently told her that she was "the best person".

Through this situation, Nadia has learnt how important it is not to have any expectations, to remain totally open-minded and persevere in each relationship. "By putting aside the judgements and the wish to distance myself that was previously so habitual, I find that I can love and support them all to find their own ways of expression." As a result, she's often startled by their intelligence and beauty – "even if it shines out for just a split second".

Nadia's account is a lovely example of a situation where we want to have good relationships with people that we find troublesome. Nadia discovered her body gave her a clear signal when she was trying to avoid or push one of her troublesome people away – she felt physical discomfort and fatigue. And she realized that her unconscious wish to avoid that discomfort was having a major effect on the quality of her relationships. As we've discussed, this body-centred awareness and sensitivity is a critical feature of learning how to deal with difficult people more wisely. However, as Nadia's example shows, to notice these subtle feelings, we need to make sure we've got a solid routine of daily practice and bring a strong intention to stay present and aware when things bear down.

The next three examples illustrate a slightly different, more introspective or self-reflective approach to dealing with troublesome people. They show what can happen when we start looking deeply at ourselves (or, as it's known in Buddhism, "turning the lamp around"). The first is an example of two people becoming mutually troublesome to each other and the mess of emotions that arise around the situation. The second illustrates what happens when we identify a blind spot in our awareness, and, with intention and practice, allow the light from our lamp of awareness to gradually expand. The third is an account of someone who, after noticing how overwhelmed she'd become by work pressure, realized the importance of relaxing, centring and re-evaluating her attitudes toward work.

Recognizing that your colleague isn't a monster

Ed works in a big city law firm and for some years served as head of his department. When Ed relinquished the role, a colleague was promoted into his old department-head position. Although Ed didn't know this colleague particularly well, he said: "I had already developed a few half-baked opinions about him as stubborn, vociferous and a complainer." Looking back, Ed can see that the seeds of their emerging troublesome relationship had already been sown at this point. Ed was judgemental of his colleague. "I didn't make time to listen to him when I was managing the team. So when it became his turn to run the department, I think my colleague saw me as a threat and actively sought to isolate me from the rest of the team." As a result, Ed felt bullied and angry. Things got bad enough that he considered leaving the firm, but the state of the economy at the time made him think twice. "So on top of my anger," he said, "I felt trapped."

It was around this time that Ed started practising Zen and began to turn his attention toward himself and cultivate a deeper sensitivity to his emotional state. In his practice he started to see and acknowledge the "tangle of his emotions", as he put it. "I became aware of the sense of outrage of finding myself in this situation and then regret that I hadn't left the company when I could have – I was hard on myself at the time." Slowly he started to see that both he and his colleague were interacting with each other from within their respective emotional knots. "We were triggering each other and bringing out the worst in each other", he said. "I probably came across as an equally troublesome person for my colleague!"

As Ed became willing to see and accept all that was arising, the knots of emotion began to loosen. "It felt like mud settling in a jug of water" – his emotions settled and quietened down slowly. Over a period of months, he began challenging some of his own "opinions and moral indignations" and trying to see things from different perspectives. "With continued practice and reflection," he said, "I realized that me and my colleague were essentially in this together – he's not a monster; he too has a family and a wife that loves him and was trying to do his best at the time."

As the tangle slowly unravelled and Ed became more accepting of what was going on, he remembers the interactions with his colleague became easier and less confrontational. He acknowledged his own role in the relationship and became open to a much more nuanced understanding of the process. "I needed to turn toward my anger and frustration and create a space in which to explore these emotions." This was a very painful process. He told me: "I started to acknowledge to myself my own historic failures of awareness and inflexibility and take responsibility for my part of the troublesome relationship."

The two of them never became good friends, but through this process Ed learnt the importance of forgiveness – to both himself and his colleague. "Forgiveness", he said, "has nothing to do with excusing their behaviour or even reconciling with them. But it's about integrating all that bad feeling and difficulty and accepting yourself and the other person for what we really are." He discovered that that means they're "in this life together, deeply connected and entwined – along with everyone else in the world".

In the end, this whole experience has helped Ed "feel a profound sense of connectivity with everyone and everything around him, even in those people we find the most difficult in our lives".

The problem isn't where you think it is

Being a freelance contractor, Julia has worked in many different companies over the years and has always found work to be a challenging environment. "I have a long history of working for bullies", she said. As a result, there were periods in the past where she'd felt totally blocked and stuck by the level of stress she was experiencing. "I ended up taking time off and being prescribed antidepressants," she said. "I would often struggle to sleep and found my cognitive mind going fuzzy and difficult to keep focused."

After she started practising Zen and bringing awareness and attention to her own mind, Julia began to notice certain patterns: "It occurred to me that some of what I had been feeling must be to do with my own attitudes and beliefs." Julia recognized that she habitually perceived herself as unimportant, so would often end up staying quiet in a meeting or taking a back seat on a project – but "when I was ignored by others or didn't get told things I became frustrated." She felt that the contrasting ambition and drive of some of her colleagues meant that they often made decisions for her, and this frustrated her even more.

Through her practice of "turning the lamp within" (enquiring into herself), she said, "I found a kind of blind spot" – something she was aware of but wasn't able to see. She describes it "like looking for something that you've lost, but only being able to search directly under the lamp"; the problem wasn't where she thought it was. So she started where she could – by acknowledging that she felt like a victim. "When a negative interaction happened, like when someone over-stepped into my territory, I recognized that all I was able to see was my own suffering." She understood that having a victim mindset meant that she would always see the problem as lying with someone else, expecting everyone else to change their behaviour. Looking back, she now sees that she may often have been a troublesome person for her colleagues too.

Slowly Julia began to recognize that problems arose when she was focused on herself and her own issues – thinking "poor me" and totally forgetting about the other person's needs. "I knew I needed to start shifting my attention away from myself to the broader picture." With this more open sphere of attention, "I began appreciating that my colleagues have separate lives, wishes and objectives, and some of my most troublesome interactions may not have had anything to do with me personally." It was about this time that things really shifted in her Zen practice: "I saw my true nature – that I'm not separate from the universe at all." She found this new perspective extremely helpful.

"Nowadays, when I'm particularly stressed, I can easily slip back into my old patterns of feeling worthless and a victim – when, for example, I'm in a meeting and resist asking a question because I think no one would be interested." But the difference is she can now more quickly recognize the tell-tale unpleasant feelings that arise with these mindsets. She is also able to see their negative effects on her creativity and thinking processes. "Although I still find it difficult to affect the trajectory of the pattern once I'm in it, I'm much more acutely aware of my own feelings and thoughts. When I recognize it early enough, I can consciously redirect my attention from the miserable inward feelings of self-pity to the broader environment and what the other people around me might want, need or feel." It gives her a sense of agency and a greater sense of freedom. "Other people can behave irresponsibly or unethically but I have more clarity and freedom to see what exactly is happening and deal with it." The workplace, she says, continues to be a wonderful practice ground since it repeatedly forces her to look at her patterns. While she can still recognize suffering arising within herself, she is committed to staying in her job. "There's still lots to learn."

Overwhelmed by demanding emails

Zarina is a music teacher at a successful city university and teaches classes to people with a wide range of ages and backgrounds. She's always been required to send out difficult and sensitive emails pertaining to things like performance and incidents of potential copying or cheating. But since the department opened up their courses to university-level students, she's found the number of difficult and demanding emails arriving from students has increased. "I now have students contacting me asking for advice and disclosing all sorts of personal issues including mental health problems."

After an incident in her department a few years ago when a particularly stressed and vulnerable student attempted suicide, she started to feel a great deal of pressure from the university to be extra mindful of how she worded her emails, with an insistence that she always stay positive and encouraging. But with students divulging personal information and asking difficult things of her, she felt like she was "sitting next to a bomb that could go off at any time".

Zarina says she appreciated "that each student is coming from different place with different issues and I wanted to be supportive in what I wrote to them, but I'm not a counsellor – it's not my job." She knew she had to avoid getting too involved. "I could do no more than send emails, but getting the right balance was difficult. I became increasingly aware that written words are easy to misunderstand, especially around sensitive topics."

Over time, Zarina started to feel more and more tired, and found less time to look after her own wellbeing. "I noticed rising feelings of irritation and anger with the situation and I started to think about quitting my job." However, because of a similar situation she'd experienced in the past, she was able to recognize these as early warning symptoms of feeling overwhelmed. "Ten years ago I'd been put in a position at work where I felt I couldn't say no and ended up stressed out. At that time, even though my mind had said yes, my body gave a clear no. It reacted strongly and I actually lost half my hair and had to buy a wig." She realized that her thoughts of wanting to quit stemmed from wanting to escape or avoid what was going on. "That was an alert; I knew I had to be careful."

In the intervening decade Zarina had established a strong meditation and yoga practice. She found her regular morning routine really helped her tune in, feel more centred and let go of her anger. "Rather than thinking, I spent the time feeling, returning to my own truth, my core." Of her yoga practice in particular, she said: "It helped me to relax, allowing my muscles and posture to return to neutral – it felt like a massage."

She began to see how the onslaught of difficult emails with enquiries and questions that needed responding to with care and sensitivity was sapping her energy. "It needed real stamina." Through her practice she was able to more closely observe how she felt and realized just how negatively she perceived herself. "I feel weak, but at the same time I thought that my practice should make me feel strong and tough." She also noticed a sense of wanting feedback or appreciation when she'd made a real effort, and the feeling of disappointment when she didn't get it. She saw how that would sap her energy even more.

"This moment-to-moment attention, enquiry and care made me aware of the constant coming and going of energy, both in the sense of energy levels within myself and the flow of energy between me and my students." She became acutely aware of her own wishes to be caring and compassionate toward her students and how difficult it was to bring that same level of care and compassion toward herself. This process has made her reflect deeply on her lifestyle and what she wants out of life. "I'm grateful that it has created a big cloud of questioning and wondering!"

As we examine our own attitudes, habits and thoughts and realize that our inner perceptions and the outer reality are different, this can lead to a deep questioning of our opinions. The following is a clear example of how doing this can dramatically change the basis of a relationship and provide lessons that can be of deep value in other difficult situations.

Keep your friends close and your enemies closer

James works in a small company. Over the past year he's noticed how often he snaps at his manager. In his view: "She has a knack of walking into my office at a moment when I'm feeling particularly stressed (having just come off a call or finished a meeting) and asking something that doesn't need an urgent answer and just as easily could be put in an email." When he's in this more vulnerable and uncollected state, her question can instigate a flash of anger. "I would impulsively lash out saying something rather childish and not thought out." Then, once the emotion has been released, he may try to backtrack and make an attempt at being friendlier.

James has noticed that "many others in my office also find her difficult, which gives me a sense of validation for my impulsive reactions". He recognizes that this knowledge adds an extra level of energy to his explosive responses. James feels a pull into getting involved in negative banter about her, but also an opposite tug from knowing he really shouldn't contribute, and the tension only adds more stress to the whole situation.

In his life, James has always struggled to adequately express himself and has a habit of holding emotions in. "I've done a lot of work in psychotherapy, and through my Zen practice I've been trying to fully acknowledge my feelings and experiment with expressing them." At this point, he saw himself as relatively inexperienced in handling strong emotions and regulating his responses – especially when overloaded by stress. In these explosive outbursts, he recognized the voice of his inner hurt child self "clumsily articulating its upset feelings".

Outside of work, James often found himself ruminating on thoughts about her – "how she's a bully, not very nice, or this or that". He added: "It was so easy to get stuck in thinking 'she's bad' – and once that opinion had formed, it would add a kind of legitimacy or energy to the hard distinction of 'she's bad'."

He found that taking time out of his day to sit on a park bench and practise stepping into a more expansive mindset really helped. "I found an increasing willingness to be with the suffering I was experiencing then and there, and not just leave work and box it up as I'd done in the past." He began trying to consider her compassionately, as a person doing her best, doing what she can according to what she knows. With time, in these more expansive moments, he was able to connect with the Buddha-nature perspective – that we're all dynamic, interconnected processes unfolding in this one universe.

He started to make a point of building interactions with her that weren't based on "her jumping on me when I wasn't prepared". He said: "I was struck by the phrase 'keep your friends close and your enemies closer' – there's so much wisdom in that!" Gradually he tried to initiate more friendly contact that wasn't just about office logistics and admin, including other aspects of their lives like family and holidays.

He said: "These days I'm still far from being equanimous." But he's learnt "not to try and engage with her questions when I'm feeling stressed". Instead, he urges her to put simple, non-urgent issues in an email for dealing with later. "But I occasionally drop the ball and lash out. It's still difficult to find that expansive compassion and kindness in the moment of anger."

In the above example, James noticed "the voice of his inner hurt child self" speaking out when his emotions ran high. With many of us, there's often a sense of shame or embarrassment when we think we've come across as childish, and it's easy to want to pretend those parts of ourselves don't exist. But, as we've discussed, denial or suppression are never the solution. However, it can be equally difficult when we see aspects of ourselves that we don't like reflected in another, as is illustrated in the following account.

When your colleague reminds you of your mother

Rose used to work in a sales team, and the colleague she sat opposite became a troublesome person for her. This woman had "extreme narcissistic tendencies and would always look down on everyone", regularly belittling her and what she was doing. However, this woman was actually good at her job and Rose suspected that this was why her negative attitude was never really addressed by the management. "What's more," Rose admitted, "I'm a habitual people-pleaser, so in those days I found it extremely difficult to confront my colleague about her behaviour." To begin with, Rose tried her best to see her as just another human being with her own fallacies and idiosyncrasies, but "that just didn't cut it". She said: "I continued to feel angry and frustrated with the situation." This was a difficult period in her life.

Rose began seeing a psychotherapist, and one of their suggestions was that she ask to move desks. The request was granted and, even though she moved just a few desks down the line, "the distance gave me some breathing room to begin a deeper enquiry into what was going on". And so: "With time I realized the things that angered me the most about my colleague were exactly those tendencies within myself that I most disliked – the belittling, 'worthier than' and know-it-all kind of attitude." With further enquiry, she saw that these were, in turn, characteristics of her mother's that she had found difficult as she was growing up. That these had become part of her and were now being reflected by her colleague she found hard. However, just seeing and accepting this allowed Rose's stance to soften. She began to frame her colleague's behaviour as something that was originating from her own inner child – Rose perceived her "as acting like a hurt seven-year-old". She said: "It dawned on me that no one acts like that without having experienced great suffering in their life." This prompted an upwelling of compassion.

Over time, Rose managed to approach her troublesome colleague and found she was able to open up to her about her own life and mother. The colleague, in turn, also opened up about her life. This act of drawing alongside each other "changed our relationship dramatically". "Unfortunately," she went on, "my colleague's behaviour didn't change, but I found I no longer became triggered by it and was able to move on." Later, she remembers feeling great empathy and sadness for the way her colleague continued to interact with other members of their team and how they reacted to her. Although Rose knew she couldn't change what was happening, her understanding and feelings of empathy allowed her to support the other members of their team.

Rose found that recognizing her colleague's troublesome behaviour as originating from her inner child gave her a way of seeing her intrinsic human nature – the fundamental nature that is shared by each of us underneath all the conditioning, pain and suffering that we experience in life.

Seeing clearly what's going on, and honestly acknowledging and accepting what we find, naturally leads to a growing sense of steadiness. This is because when we learn to accept things as they are, we're no longer bound by the desperate wishes and aversions of the ego. This leads to a feeling of groundedness and steadfastness, such that even in the face of difficulty and emotional turmoil, we can remain centred, knowing that even if it feels unpleasant, it's okay. But finding equanimity and staying steady isn't easy. The following example shows how sometimes events can rock the boat to such a degree that we lose touch with that balance and stability, even when we're familiar with its presence.

Finding stillness beneath the tumult

Kumar held a managerial position at work and went through a period of having to make unpopular decisions. Sometimes, he remembers, "this was met with disgruntled acceptance, and other times with outright conflict and verbal aggression". Kumar found himself feeling stressed and unsettled and started having difficulty sleeping.

Through his established mindfulness and meditation practice, he was able to bring awareness and sensitivity to what was happening. "At the height of my emotional difficulties, my feelings had felt diffuse and difficult to grasp in my awareness." With continued practice, he was able to bring things into more focus: "My perception of my internal state became more concrete, with sharp edges and more substance to it." He felt the intense frustration at the situation at work and disappointment in himself, but the increased definition of his feelings, he said, "strangely made them easier to relate to".

"My emotional landscape had for many years been steady and quiet, but this situation felt like an enormous explosion in that landscape that had produced a big black cloud that obscured everything else." In staying with this image, Kumar realized that "although it appeared at first like there was nothing else but the swirling, turbulent black cloud, the quiet empty landscape was actually still there in the background". He recognized: "I could sink beneath the tumult of emotions to find that still steadiness that had always been there."

Although it took some time and practice, he was able to begin regaining touch with this steadiness in his work environment. Even though emotions were still running high, he found this feeling of background stability allowed him to deal with the situation and relate to his colleagues in a much more balanced and calm way.

CHAPTER 7
FRIEND BUDDHAS

On one occasion, the Buddha's cousin and close attendant, Ananda, was sitting next to him in the company of friends and family. Ananda remarked: "This is half of the holy life, lord: admirable friendship, admirable companionship, admirable camaraderie." The Buddha replied: "Don't say that, Ananda. Admirable friendship, admirable companionship, admirable camaraderie is actually the whole of the holy life. When a monk has admirable people as friends, companions, and comrades, he can be expected to develop and pursue the noble eightfold path."[13] [14]

In this short response, the Buddha emphasises the central importance of *sangha* – our friends, family and people we spend time with. Friendship and companionship give us fun and laughs, shared experiences, support through thick and thin and guidance to keep us on the straight and narrow. But inevitably, even your closest friends can rub you up the wrong way now and then. This is part of their role as a friend. They're there to challenge you when it's needed, and it's your responsibility to take those opportunities to learn and develop.

At times it can be difficult to appreciate that you also have a role in creating the difficulty you perceive. I know that from my own experience. For example, we might see ourselves as being an exemplary friend, and think that whatever is happening can only be the other person's fault. But even if you're completely blind to your own part in the troublesome relationship, you can be sure you must be bringing something. A relationship is co-created – after all, it takes two electric plates coming together to create a spark. It's essential we develop a willingness to be open and question our behaviour. Even if you don't know what the matter is, we can still ask if there's anything we can do. It's through this honesty and humility that deep change happens.

In the following, we'll see a variety of situations where various people's friends became troublesome. In the first one, we'll hear from Paula, who initially found the overt friendliness of a new acquaintance overbearing. However, the intensity of the situation they were in kept her having to face her difficulties until, one day, she saw how much she'd been resisting and holding on, and realized it's okay to let her guard down. This realization became an important lesson that she's been able to apply in other situations. It has also led her toward a deeper examination of her relationship with her mother and her feelings of duty and responsibility. In doing so, some of the roots of her guarded behaviour have started to come to light.

Coming to terms with softness, patience and generosity

Paula first met Erin on their yoga teacher training course some years ago. Right away, Paula started to get frustrated and annoyed by Erin's soft, gentle demeanour. In the first few days of their training retreat, Paula remembers her reaching out, often in non-verbal terms, offering help and friendship. However, Paula said, "I just didn't want the interaction – I remember feeling I wanted to be left alone. She was always smiling at me and I felt she was trying to push kindness on me."

As time went on, Paula started to notice that she was feeling annoyed at herself for being irritated with Erin. "I could see other people really warming to her – everyone else was happy with her offers of help." But, at least initially, she didn't know why she felt so annoyed. As time went on, she realized it was connected to a feeling of defensiveness and a resistance to letting her guard down.

A turning point came about halfway through the course. Paula remembers showing up to the class one morning a little early, and found herself alone with Erin. "I felt differently at that moment, and this was an opportunity to roll with that." Paula offered to make her tea. "It felt nice to do that." She commented: "I was tired that morning, so I think this helps wear us down to the heart of things. My mask was down and I felt safe because there was no audience."

As the days went on, Paula was able to let her guard down more and more. "During the rest of the course I found myself moving physically closer to her and starting to smile back." She realized Erin wasn't trying to push anything on her. "Actually she was just being present like an open book, and I came to realize it was an honour to be in the presence of someone so kind, generous and selfless." Since the training course, her and Erin have stayed in touch and met up fairly regularly. Paula describes her as a strong influence and guide (probably mostly unknowingly, she said). "Erin has become a thread which has woven into my life and it feels like the best gift."

Since that time, Paula said, "I've noticed other situations where I do this – like in classes and on retreats that I'm leading. Students move close to me – I feel them starting to lean on me – and then I begin to want to move away from that pressure. I appreciate there's something in me they want to be near to – and for that I feel happy – but I have this reservation to opening the door fully."

Her years of Zen practice have allowed her to see some of the reasons why she might feel like this. "I've been brought up to be independent, confident and capable. When I struggled at anything as a child, my parents always urged me on, saying 'come on, you can do this'. As a result I think I've come to see softness and patience as a weakness." She told me she thinks her walls come up when people are being kind, and that's when she starts to feel annoyed with their softness and generosity.

In recent years she's seen this pattern reflected back to her through her relationship with her mum. "My mum's always seen herself as independent and capable, and this has a lot to do with her upbringing. But as she's become older and frailer, she still perceives herself as being as capable as she ever was." Because of this discrepancy, her mother gets frustrated and impatient. "This has led to a great deal of anxiety. I have to be this capable, supportive figure for her – but she won't accept my offers of help. When I offer solutions, they're either ignored or batted back." As a result, Paula has noticed a new pattern. "Because I can't change things for my mum and she won't take my help, I've noticed that I've started to throw myself into being a helper for others!"

Over the years, her Zen practice has taught her to be kinder toward herself when she notices her emotions, habits and patterns. "I've learnt that rather than getting drawn in, I need to take a step back and listen before I take any actions. Over time, I've become less emotionally caught-up." She's also grateful for her ongoing difficult relationship with her mother. "It was my feelings about her that sent me in the direction of Zen in the first place."

While some people like Paula may habitually resist the kindness and support of friends, others may find themselves in a situation of craving friendship that isn't necessarily forthcoming. The following example from my own life illustrates the anguish that I felt when wanting to be accepted into a pre-existing friendship group and the resulting realization of shared humanity.

Cliquey behaviour

Not long ago I started a new hobby and began attending the associated club quite regularly. After some time, when I was around some of the long-standing members, I started to get a sense of being on the outside of an established social group that wasn't particularly open to newcomers. I saw this as cliquey behaviour, and I recognized the unpleasant feeling I got from a number of similar situations in the past. Despite multiple attempts at being friendly with this group, I felt an air of unwelcome and a sense that I was unimportant to them. These few members would sometimes blank me when I said hello and I realized they would often meet up afterwards for a drink without telling or inviting me (or indeed anyone else). They often made in-jokes, making no attempt to explain them to me; I sometimes got the feeling they had a special language they used between themselves that I didn't know.

I perceived that they thought I was unimportant – and, unconsciously, I took on that belief. As a result I started shrinking away from them, feeling uncomfortable in myself and reluctant to make any new attempts to connect with any of the individuals. I recognize now that this is a habit pattern of mine in these circumstances. I became aware that I'd started to ruminate on how difficult they were being and how much of an outsider I felt. Even after years of Zen practice, it took me a long time to remember I could use the arising of these thoughts as a prompt or reminder to myself to try and create a more expansive, accepting attitude. I did my best to fully acknowledge and accept my shrinking-away behaviour, understanding that it's just a psychological protection mechanism against getting hurt. I saw that some part of me still really wanted to be accepted and part of the in-group. By also bringing this "want" into the light of my awareness, seeing it for what it was and giving it space to be, I found that gave me the choice not to let it dictate my behaviour.

Slowly I regained confidence around this group. I found that when I interacted with any one of them on a one-to-one basis I could find moments of true connection and friendliness. This helped me see that any cliquey behaviour I came across didn't arise from any sense of malice on their part. With further refection I remembered past instances when I myself was part of an established social group and the tempting intoxication of feeling "in" when others are "out".

As I brought this, too, into my awareness and did my best not to judge it, I began to appreciate how this group and I share an intrinsic human nature. This situation became another pointer that, yes, on the surface we behave in all sorts of ways because of our conditioning, experiences and tendencies, but underneath all that there's a shared wholeness that's always been there – if we just give ourselves the chance to see it.

Problems with friends can arise in a moment or can bubble below the surface for a long time – particularly with more distant friends or acquaintances. The following is an example of a simmering relationship that exploded into an angry confrontation brought on by a longer-than-usual period of closeness. This release of emotions turned out to have a liberating and healing effect on the relationship. This demonstrates the value of getting deeply held emotions and grievances out into the open, even if they've been held for a long time.

An unavoidable explosion

Ever since Simon first met his wife's best friend Trudy, 15 years ago, they've had a difficult relationship. Simon's wife and Trudy have been close since they were children and have stayed close as they both got married and had children. Simon finds Trudy "totally humourless, moody and always wanting things to go her way". When their families got together, Simon remembers, "I would always lay down my weapons and laugh things off just to keep the peace". But over the years she grated on him more and more and he began to resent the way she bullied and spoke down to him.

Recently Simon's family spent the holidays with Trudy and her family at their country home. Their arrival, he recalled, sparked a memory of a flare-up during their last meeting, and this "immediately set me on edge". Simon had a habit of forgetting to give cards for birthdays and other events, so when Trudy realized that he hadn't got a card for his wife on her birthday, "she started laying into me". He said: "I could feel she wanted to start a fight, and, for the sake of the peace, I made a monstrous effort not to go there." Despite his efforts though, she "lit the touch paper when she compared me to her own husband, saying he always gives her a card". The two of them exploded. Simon recalls how they were like two balls of anger, letting rip all the pent-up emotions from the past. "I told her how I thought she was a bully and liked to dominate people." She said he behaved like he was better than everybody else and treated everyone like he was a prince. At the end of the argument, Simon felt like a quivering wreck. "I went to find my wife to tell her we were leaving."

His wife managed to calm him down and the next day the two of them avoided each other. After a few more days of cooling down, Simon approached Trudy and said he was sorry. "I was able to describe my anger at her, about how unfair it felt to be forced to creep around on egg shells, about how I felt she'd treated me with disrespect." Simon went on: "I felt I brought equal value to the group, and cared just as much, even though I might not show it in the same way." They agreed that they both have certain boundaries that need to be respected and that they each express love in different ways. "This was a real turning point in our relationship." Now, some months later, he's never got on with her so well.

Simon found the initial explosion and follow-up conversation liberating, as the pressure that had built up over all the years was fully released. "I'm not sure we could've realistically had that conversation any earlier." Looking back, he thought it probably needed honesty sooner from both sides. "I could have tried to be more tolerant of the way she was – I remember often talking about her behind her back, letting off steam to my mates, expressing my emotions to the wrong person in the wrong way." But the reality is that they live far apart and don't see each other that often. "The behaviour habits had been building for 15 years and, of course, there's a tremendous resistance to starting an honest conversation when we've got together for one of our children's birthdays or for Christmas." For the short times they were together, "it was easier just to suck it up". Simon said: "Presumably it was the fact that we were together this time for a longer period than normal that forced our hands."

Through this process, Simon realized just how strongly he disliked being misunderstood and talked down to. He realized that this most likely had its roots in his childhood. "I was the youngest of my siblings and cousins and had always felt like the runt of the litter." Although this episode has shown Simon aspects of himself that he doesn't like – the vindictive, angry and defensive parts and the part that craves for recognition for his contributions within the family – through his Zen practice, he says, "I've been able to bring a sense of self-compassion and acceptance toward myself".

He's also found ways of bringing that same compassion to his wife's friend. "In the angry and hurt state all I saw was an ogre – a monster causing problems, not caring about anyone else and revelling in a punishment mindset." But with time he's come to recognize that, deep down, she's actually quite an unhappy individual. His anger and loathing has transformed into sadness and empathy, particularly as he recognizes "how all the negativity and physical tension must be taking its toll on her system". He told me: "Underneath the leathery hide of anger and meanness that I've come to see, I've been able to find glimpses of a nice person, and I've worked hard on starting to make room for more transparent moments in our relationship."

The following example reminds me of a metaphor that's often used in Zen to describe what happens in your practice when you're in close contact with other people (like the monks who traditionally lived in a temple). Living in close proximity to others is seen as like being in a rock tumbler. In the beginning the rocks go in with sharp, jagged edges

— the young monks have many preconceptions, opinions, habits and beliefs conditioned by their past experiences and suffering. For example, my teacher remembers that in his first few years of living in a monastery with almost no privacy at all, he developed a death wish on almost everyone there! But slowly, through the process of banging up against everyone else in the tumbler-monastery, all those rough edges started to get smoothed out. Ideally the young monks come out the other end as beautifully polished jewels. The following is an example of someone bumping up against a fellow member of their meditation group, not in a monastery but in normal daily life. With help from their teacher, they learnt to see their reactions as a reflection of where they're stuck in their own habits and preconceptions, and as an indicator of where they can let go.

A long series of life lessons from a troublesome Buddha

A few years ago Luca joined a meditation group and attended frequently. Gradually he became a central member of the group, and it wasn't long before he started to find Olive, one of the other members of the group, particularly difficult. Olive, he remembers, "was generally lovely, kind and dedicated to the group". However, various aspects of her behaviour irritated and grated on Luca. Her dedication meant she volunteered to do many things, but, he said, "I got the sense that she felt undervalued and she'd often express to me that she thought her efforts were going unrecognized." Luca also felt she had a negative attitude toward some others in the group and would often criticize them behind their backs. "It was many little things I noticed about Olive and her behaviour that, over time, created a cumulative negative effect that I found increasingly difficult."

Luca remembers various occasions when he approached the group's main teacher feeling exasperated and asking how he could continue working with her. Luca asked him if he was aware of her behaviour and, if so, why didn't he say anything?

Luca felt "the teacher had always been patient with Olive and never expressed any kind of judgement". Despite Luca wanting to feel validated in his feelings, the teacher would neither confirm nor deny whether he had noticed the same things or whether he thought they were grounded in reality.

The teacher reassured Luca that this was one of the purposes of being in a group like theirs. He encouraged him to use this as a wonderful opportunity to practise acceptance, tolerance and patience, and to persevere in trying to understand where she was coming from. He also suggested that he start looking into where his frustration and irritation originated. "I began to soften my attitude and look to see what I could learn from each encounter with Olive." He realized that he thought the sole problem was the way she was behaving, and that he was playing no part in creating the concomitant frustration. Gradually he realized that this was a one-sided view. "I recognized a whole host of judgemental thoughts and solidified opinions, including that she 'should' be different and act differently and that she ought to look harder at some of her issues." He could also trace back some of his frustration to when she stated something about the world (be that about people, attitudes or events) that he just didn't see that way.

Luca made it a point to ask Olive more about her history and background. "Slowly, I was able see things a little more from her point of view and understand her behaviour, given her past and her own suffering." Even if he couldn't understand it, he "became more able to just accept her for who she was." This process of softening and acceptance took some years, and he can see there's certainly still further to go. "Now and then, I still notice that rising irritation at something she says or does, but can see both her actions and my reactions in a much broader, compassionate light." Luca is deeply grateful to Olive for providing him with such a long series of life lessons in how to approach troublesome behaviour and how to use his reactions as a mirror to show him where he's still stuck and holding on. He said: "Olive is a true Buddha that appeared to me in a troublesome form."

CHAPTER 8
NEIGHBOUR AND HOUSEMATE BUDDHAS

Living in close proximity to others can become challenging. If nothing else, it can just be difficult to avoid someone who gets up your nose or grates on you. Sometimes it's nothing they've actually done; we often get annoyed with people for just being themselves, for their innate personality or individual quirks!

Neighbourly disputes frequently start with the tiniest of things, but, if we're not careful, can quickly escalate into massive problems. I knew someone that lived in an apartment block with his wife and three-year-old toddler. They thought it was outrageous when the downstairs neighbour asked them to stop their child clomping across the floor (as that's what it sounded like to them). Apart from covering their whole flat with rubber matting, they felt there was nothing they could do. After repeated requests, the whole thing blew out of proportion when their neighbours called the police. After that, it stopped being about the noise and became more about each other's stubbornness and refusal to accept each other's point of view.

When you feel like you're "in the right", there's a huge temptation to dig your heels in and dismiss even the potential of compromise. We end up holding onto an idea for its own sake, and going to extreme lengths to prove that we're right or win the argument (like taking your neighbour to court over a boundary dispute of a few inches). But why do we do this, when we know it causes so much suffering? Because when our fragile sense of identity feels threatened, rationality quickly goes out the window. We do everything we can to make sure our ego feels safe.

The negative feelings and stress resulting from an ongoing dispute can cause all sorts of bodily responses, including tension, digestive problems, headaches and nausea. For your own health, anything you can do that might help you let go of that indignation, resentment, frustration or anger is of great benefit. Sometimes it's just about knowing when it's time to remove yourself from the situation. Other times you may need to do something more direct, like going for a long walk, going for a massage, doing certain forms of yoga or practising more mindfulness meditation.

The Dalai Lama once said: "To be aware of a single shortcoming within oneself is more useful than to be aware of a thousand in someone else."[15] This is what our honest and open mindfulness practice does. It brings to our attention our conditioned reactions, our opinions, fixed ideas and habitual ego-protection mechanisms. It shows us our shortcomings – and gives us the opportunity to choose new ways of acting that lead away from suffering and toward kindness and compassion. We can try seeing things from the other person's point of view, give them the benefit of the doubt or respond with a kind act (for example, giving them some kind of peace offering).

In the end, it can make a world of difference if you've already developed a friendly (or even just cordial) relationship with your neighbour or housemate before any issues might arise. There's wisdom in the old Chinese proverb: "A good neighbour is a priceless treasure." Problems with a troublesome person almost never escalate so seriously if you already have a positive relationship with them.

The first two examples below illustrate what happens when we become aware of the machinations of our minds, how they quickly jump to conclusions and form impressions and perceptions. First, we'll hear from Patrick about a parking situation that got on his wick. Through his sincere enquiry, he was able to observe as his mind wove so many judgemental stories around the situation and attempted to assign blame. As he examined his thoughts and assumptions further, he was able to find new levels of acceptance, understanding and contentment with the situation. In the second example, we'll see how Dele's initial impressions of his housemate were shattered as he gradually saw more clearly what his housemate was like. As he persevered with their relationship, he was able to reframe his difficulties and transform the situation.

Parking in half a space

Patrick lives in the third house from the end of a street with restricted, residents-only parking. Parking is available in a long, undivided strip, parallel to the direction of the street (as is commonly found in UK towns). On an average day, Patrick's neighbour arrives back from work earlier than him and parks his car directly in front of his house. This leaves room for about two-and-a-half more cars before the end of the parking bay. When Patrick gets home, he often finds only half a space available, so ends up having to park on a different street.

"Each time this happened, I would feel angry that they'd effectively taken up two spaces and start blaming my neighbour for being so selfish. If they would pull forward just a little bit!" However, his years of meditation practice allowed him to consciously observe that inner process of judging and searching for blame. He remembers thinking "they shouldn't do that and should be more considerate", but there was a voice inside him that said "they're probably not attempting to be inconsiderate and doing it just so I have nowhere to park". As he noticed this polyphony of thoughts with all the "shoulds" and "probablys", he remembers "starting to laugh at how my mind manages to wind itself up like that". Later, he noticed that on the drive home some part of him would be hoping for the usual parking issue and for the usual set of judgemental thoughts to arise, just so he could laugh at himself!

Despite the parking problem not being Patrick's fault, he realized that his mind was constantly seeking a way of being involved. "No matter how much I attempted to just be with the situation, my mind would find some way of also having a say, trying to cognitively work out or justify the situation, or assign blame so I can feel blameless." Patrick recognized this as an automated tendency.

He said he began trying to view his inner voice as "friendly and well-intentioned, but just not very well educated – like a child offering simple, naïve advice". This gave him a new way of acknowledging and accepting his judgemental thoughts. "I could see them not on the level of an intrusion to be got rid of, but instead as something to just be patient and curious about, as you would with a child." As a result he started to recognize those same judging, blaming tendencies in many other places in his life. He remembers asking himself: "Is this a pattern that's serving me well or pulling me away from my commitment to the precepts[16] and the practice of right thought and right speech?"[17]

Patrick said he's grateful to his neighbour for continuing to park as he does and for giving him so many opportunities to look so closely at himself. "Seeing the mind's workings so clearly is more valuable than winning the argument of who parks where." For him, this was a mini-revelation.

If the time arose and it felt appropriate, Patrick said he would certainly consider having a conversation with his neighbour about the situation. "I'm sure after my revelation I would be far less emotional about whatever I might say, and might even have a sense of humour about it all. But I also think that bringing it up out of the blue would only be self-serving. I've managed thus far, and talking about it would, at best, only benefit me and, at worst, make my neighbour feel terrible for all those years of inefficient parking."

Reframing your initial judgements

Dele has been flat-sharing with a woman for about six months. From their first conversation, he knew they weren't on the same wavelength. His initial impressions were that she was cold and insensitive, and in the first few months he struggled to relate to her rather guarded nature. They were different people with no obvious shared interests.

At this point, Dele had been practising Zen for a decade or so. He said: "My practice has taught me that first impressions aren't always what they seem." Over the first few months, their rather awkward domestic conversations about things like cooking and cleaning became little windows through which he started to see her in new ways. He was also able to see her professional side since she worked at home dealing with customer complaints. He admitted: "Witnessing her repeatedly dealing with angry and frustrated customers in a consistent, professional and calm manner amazed me. I started to see her apparent coldness as actually the characteristic of a practical, capable and level-headed person." He marvelled at how unfazed by issues and good at adapting she appeared to be. "I can see she's stronger than me in so many ways."

Through his practice, he told me he was able to bring a level of awareness to his initial judgements and difficulties in their relationship, and have a willingness to stick with things without immediately running away. "This space and clarity allowed me to reframe my perception of her." He now feels more comfortable to continue sharing a flat with this woman.

Dele reflected on where his practice had brought him: "I find every encounter with a person or situation that stirs up frustration, annoyance and suffering provides a renewed urgency for me to deepen my practice. Brushing up against difficulty in life stimulates me into action and gives me the motivation to try and see whatever is arising as clearly as possible."

In the next two examples, we'll encounter a much more body-centred response to the difficulties of troublesome people. We'll hear how a dispute over building a sun shade sent Alan headlong into making a difficult decision he knew would anger his neighbour, and how that caused a painful build-up of tension in his body. After discovering a technique for letting go of that physical tension, Alan found he was able to communicate more clearly from his heart and gradually rebuild the relationship with his neighbour. In the account after that, we'll hear from Scott whose difficult and clingy housemate frequently distracted him from his peaceful meditation practice. The ensuing fury at being pulled away from these pleasurable states became the catalyst that encouraged Scott to look more closely at what was going on. Scott came to see his anger as a sign that he wasn't fully accepting his housemate and the situation as it was. This became a visceral lesson for Scott that there's a great deal more to spiritual practice than just achieving tranquil and peaceful states of mind.

Seeking shade from the sun

Alan met Lucia, the troublesome Buddha of this example, when she was a student on a mindfulness course he taught some years ago. Lucia loved the course and got on very well. A couple of years ago Alan, his wife and little baby moved into a ground-floor flat in a private gated community, and it turned out that Lucia lived in the apartment upstairs.

In this community, the grounds belong to everybody and there are no strict rules on what people can or can't do. Alan wanted to build a wooden structure on the terrace outside his flat in order to provide some shade from the summer sun, so solicited for agreement from his neighbours. He made a particular point of asking Lucia since he would need to nail some of the beams to her outside wall. She initially agreed.

However, it was only once Alan had bought all the materials and they'd been delivered that Lucia told him she'd had second thoughts. "She anticipated that her washing might catch on the wooden beams and she was worried she wouldn't be able to see the garden as much as she used to." Alan appealed to her, describing how much of a difference it would make to his wife and little baby who really suffer in the hot, sunny flat. He suggested that "if she could fold her sheets one more time, there would be no danger". She remained unconvinced.

Alan debated whether he should go ahead or not. His father had contributed a lot toward the cost of the materials and he felt responsible. He was incredibly torn, on one hand caring for Lucia and her feelings and wanting to be a good neighbour, and on the other appreciating the needs of his wife and little baby. "I became aware of a great deal of physical tension in my body – and even talking about it right now, I can feel tension rising in my chest and abdomen." The unpleasantness of the tension, he said, encouraged him to "live outside his body".

Alan felt he had "stretched out his hand as much as he could and there was still no solution". He said: "In the end I had to throw myself into that contradiction. I made the decision to go ahead with the building knowing that would cause Lucia suffering." Understandably, Lucia wasn't happy. He remembers her expressing her feelings in bursts of fiery anger. Alan, of course, apologized, but said he had already bought all the materials based on the fact that she had originally said yes.

"I knew there was no evil intent in her actions, she just didn't want to be taken advantage of. In my quiet meditation time I was able to recognize the shared humanity between us." Alan felt that they were both just trying to do their best given the situation and background – but admits this perspective hadn't always been at the forefront of his mind.

After noticing how physically tense his body became during this whole episode, a big discovery for Alan was the practice of shaking. He has found this to be tremendously useful in releasing the built-up tension, helping him let go and process his feelings of nervousness and trepidation. Reflecting now, he said: "I've found a huge difference between approaching a troublesome situation with a closed body, closed attitude and unaware of my physical tensions, and going in with an open body and a receptive, open mind with full awareness of how my body reacts to the difficulty."

After he discovered this tension-releasing technique, he found it much easier when he encountered her in the hallway. He's been able to speak more easily from his heart, asking her how she was doing with sincerity and honesty. Slowly, he said, he's been able to build up his relationship with her again.

Leave me to do my important spiritual practice

When Scott was at university, he lived in a large shared house and had already been practising Zen for some years. Not long after he moved in, one of his housemates became clingy. "I wanted things to go smoothly and everyone to get along, but this chap just couldn't keep himself to himself. He followed me around the house and would try to talk to me at every opportunity. He would get up on his soap box explaining his theories on all sorts of things and why he didn't like this or that, going off on long tangents."

Over time it got worse. "When this chap didn't have anything to do, he would look for me. He would frequently interrupt my meditation just to get me to listen – and I couldn't interject or challenge his perspective." He said he thought he wasn't on the same plane of reality. Scott later found out he had schizophrenia.

Scott started hiding away and taking long walks just to get away from him. When he was alone, Scott would find himself anxiously wondering "where is he?" "I got so angry with him and was unable to let it go." Scott said that in his meditation practice at the time he was regularly reaching states of beautiful peace and serenity, and this guy was "stirring the waters" and bringing him out of those pleasurable states. "I saw him getting in the way of me doing my 'important spiritual practice' – and I didn't think anger had any part in that." As time went on, he said the anger was tearing him apart. "It was torture."

Over time it became quite clear to him that being angry wasn't the path out of this. "I tried everything I could to get away from it, but I realized the only thing that works is to face it – to go completely into it." The only path was to acknowledge and fully accept him and his illness, and the effect he was having – "to be okay with him exactly the way he was". Scott went on: "Over time I came to see my anger as a sign that I was trying to escape, not fully accepting him as he was. Each time I didn't accept him, that created more suffering." As he did this, Scott began to see and appreciate this man's own suffering. "Eventually I got to a place where I could love him."

At some point, his housemate became very depressed and threatened to burn down the house. "At that point we tried to get him on a train back to his parents, but he ran away to the police. Then, in the police station, he flipped out, yelling and screaming, and again ran out. Eventually the police caught him and took him to the psychiatric hospital." He finally ended up back with his parents.

Much later, the chap came back to the house with his mum to say goodbye. Scott said: "He was much better and I could tell how much she loved him." When his mum realized how things had been living in the house, she understood he couldn't do it and it wasn't right for him. "I appreciated for the first time how hard it was for him to have been away without his mum."

Now, Scott understands. "I'm so grateful for how he helped me face my anger and learn how to accept. Without such an intense experience I would never have seen that I had those dark places, and he helped me bring them into the light more clearly." It was only after he left and the intensity of emotions had subsided that Scott could see this fellow's true Buddha-nature.

The final two accounts in this chapter illustrate what happens when we're able to open our heart and connect more directly to a sense of compassion for our troublesome person. As we've mentioned, this is often hard to do in the midst of strong feelings of irritation, anger or outrage. In both these examples, it needed them to step away from the situation and intentionally practice openness and loving kindness. The second example shows how one sometimes needs to be compassionate with oneself before being able to extend that to the troublesome person. Sometimes it takes a sustained intention to be kind and compassionate for it to truly manifest in a difficult relationship. However, the effort is always worth it for what it can teach us about ourselves and how it can shift the basis of our relationships both with ourselves and the difficult other.

Opening the gates

Fabia used to live in a large shared house. It didn't take long before she started to get annoyed with most of her housemates. But one particular woman stood out as the most irritating. "She spoke too loudly and seemed like a real goody-goody." Initially, Fabia tried her best to simply accept this woman and hold back from saying anything. She said she was worried that she'd be a "bad Buddhist" if she expressed her negative feelings and actually told her how difficult she found her behaviour. After a period of carrying around all this frustration, she said: "I realized I'd started to hate this person, essentially for doing nothing wrong – for just being who she was."

Slowly, Fabia purposefully tried "to open my awareness to this woman's behaviour – and to her loud voice in particular". She said: "In my meditation practice I would imagine my body being made of gates, and what it would be like to consciously open those gates." In her encounters with her, she tried to let her voice soak through her without any judgement. "Something hit me like a thunderbolt – I felt a kind of physical click inside, like being hit on the chest." She went on: "In my meditation practice afterwards, a whole bunch of personal stuff came up about my own life and attitudes and I burst out crying with love for this person." The decision to let this troublesome person in, whether they were in direct interaction or not, felt like a profound shift.

Now, Fabia feels grateful to this woman for annoying her. This situation gave her an opportunity to examine her attitudes toward being a Buddhist, and to realize that harbouring negative feelings only made things worse. "It taught me that if I'm able to notice my frustrations and not resist or deny them, then things don't have to build up to explosion point. It showed me how to open my gates and let people in." Fabia knows that, over the years, encounters with people like this woman have gradually taught her how to have open, honest and fulfilling relationships with people of all types – difficult or otherwise.

Living in a garden of resentment

Andrew first met Gary when they were at university and they quickly became good friends. Andrew was the best man at his wedding and godfather to his first child. A few years later, Andrew moved into a room in Gary's house and stayed there as a lodger for eight years. He told me: "Over that time a rather unhealthy pattern emerged in our relationship." Andrew found Gary increasingly difficult. Looking back now, Andrew said: "I felt all the judgements and criticisms I had of myself were kept in place, or even bolstered, by being around Gary." He felt that the dynamic of their relationship helped him to betray his own truth and that pattern become entrenched over those eight years.

About five years ago Andrew moved out. He remembers it being a traumatic time and he felt anxious to part ways, but also a sense of relief to "be out of the clutches of that relationship dynamic". In the years that followed, Andrew was aware of how he continued to resent his old friend for how he had behaved and treated him. "It became a persistent and enduring problem, even though I didn't have any more contact with him."

Andrew continued: "A storehouse of resentment and bitterness had built up inside me. As those negative thoughts arose, particularly in my meditation practice, I knew not to believe them for terribly long. But they just kept on coming up again and again." He said it felt to him like living in a garden of resentment, surrounded by voraciously growing plants. "I was constantly snipping off new shoots with no end in sight to this gardening work." He gradually recognized that the problem didn't lie with Gary, but just that "he had provoked an underlying and pre-existing wound in me".

Through his meditation practice, Andrew began to nurture an attitude of compassion toward himself. "Whenever I got into the 'who's to blame' mindset, I would drop the word 'kindness' into my experience." He saw how this kindness had an all-encompassing, 360-degree aspect to it. "It would apply to all the resentfulness, all the shoulds and shouldn'ts about how I needed to fix things or change things; it would apply to Gary, to me and to everything." By doing this, he noticed things shifted from being all about his suffering, to just suffering. "All the problems dissolved into kindness."

During a recent Zen retreat focused on the four boundless meditations,[18] Andrew was able to dedicate many hours of practice in applying compassion and loving kindness to this particular fixation, and he "found that incredibly healing". He was also able to find a "palpable sense of joy for Gary and his wife on the arrival of their fourth child" – who had been born while Andrew was living with them. Up to that point, Andrew said, he had only felt resentment. He remembers finding a deep sense of interconnection – of having a "smile without anything between mine and their smile" and an "intuitive sense that their joy was my joy – and that was just one joy shared by all".

This experience has instilled a feeling of trust in Andrew that this universal joy is always there. "Although the thoughts and feelings of resentment and bitterness still come up, I now know that this joy is never far away. When the inner dialogue turns toward assessing whether he was bad or good, or whether he exploited me or not, or whose fault it was, there's a relief or satisfaction in knowing that, from the perspective of our true nature, it doesn't matter. It's all the same."

Experience has shown Andrew that it's difficult to settle while the attention is taken up by the busy mind – with its constant "flitting between thoughts and storylines". Whereas "with the attention focused in the body, things settle much quicker". Andrew reflected on his experience: "As I've been able to stay with the physical sensations in the body, noticing them but being okay with them, I've noticed that what was personal suffering becomes impersonal suffering, not tethered to any particular person." Like this, he's been able to develop a more peaceful relationship to suffering in general and engage with the much wider, shared source of suffering in the world.

CHAPTER 9
PARTNER BUDDHAS

Prior to his life as an ascetic and monk, the Buddha was a prince in a small state in northern India with a wife and child. By all accounts he dearly loved his wife and confided in her as he began wrangling with the questions of what life is and why people suffer. In the end, his overriding urge to find enlightenment led him down a solitary path away from his wife, but he certainly took with him a great deal of what he learnt during those years of married life.

In the *Samajivina Sutta*, we find a short account of the Buddha talking to a married couple about the qualities that make a successful relationship. The couple are the parents of Nakula, one of the Buddha's original disciples. As they sat together, Nakula's father Nakulapita said to the Buddha: "Lord, ever since Nakulamata, as a young girl, was brought to me to be my wife, when I was just a young boy, I am not conscious of being unfaithful to her, even in mind, much less in body. We want to see each other, not only in the present life but also in the life to come." After that, Nakulamata also spoke to the Buddha and echoed the same words and sentiments.

They were asking him how they should live if they wanted their relationship to flourish. The Buddha responded by saying: "A husband and wife should be in tune with each other in conviction, in tune in virtue, in tune in generosity and in tune in discernment. Then they will see one another not only in the present life but also in the life to come. Husband and wife, both of them having conviction, being responsive, being restrained, living by the Dharma, addressing each other with loving words, they benefit in manifolds ways. To them comes bliss."[19]

Of all the skills needed for a successful partnership, the Buddha taught that attunement is the most important – both attunement to yourself and to one another. He then splits this attunement into four different areas.

- Being in tune with each other in conviction – an intention to walk the same road, to have the same orientation within life and perhaps the same belief system
- Being in tune in virtue – a harmonious sense of what seems true or right to the two partners, a shared morality
- Being in tune in generosity – being compatible in the levels, types and attitudes around giving to others and being generous
- Being in tune in discernment – seeing and judging things in a similar or like-minded way

It's a beautiful ideal, and it's our responsibility as a partner to strive toward that ideal – but in practice things don't always look like this. Here it's helpful to again make the comparison with monks living in a monastery and the rock-tumbler metaphor mentioned previously. In these terms, living with a partner can be seen as being in a two-person monastery or a two-rock tumbler. Yes, each bump and knock is painful – sometimes painful – but they are all opportunities to learn, grow and smooth off your jagged edges.

Just as rock tumblers need to keep tumbling, we need to continuously refine our attunement, or to recognize that we've come out of tune and re-attune with each other. This is the action of polishing. Our partner can help us learn and develop – in our nature as an individual, but also (and this is important) together as a couple in a relationship. Often you hear of someone looking for a partner who can "complete them" – as if they are a semi-circle looking for another semi-circle to create a full circle. Equally often, when someone is in a relationship, I hear them use the expression "my other half" when referring to their partner – but is becoming someone's other half really something to aspire to? If we search for existential happiness or completeness in something outside ourselves (be that a partner or indeed anything), then we're surely setting up the conditions for suffering.

Zen master Thich Nhat Hanh talks about being in a partnership as like two gardens coming together. Each one of us contains the seeds of weeds like anger, fear, discrimination and jealousy, but also of beautiful flowers like compassion, understanding and love. If we water the seeds of suffering, they will sprout into plants of pain and hate, but if we water the seeds of compassion, they will sprout into beautiful flowers of love and kindness. We must first master the practice of selective watering in our own garden. Only then do we have enough wisdom to help water the flowers in our partner's garden.

The symbolism within the Zen wedding ceremony encapsulates this very well. At the beginning, the two to be wed approach the altar from the left and right, each holding two lit candles – one red and one white. These candles represent the opposites within themselves – their elements of yin and yang, or dark and light if you like. Each has in front of them a medium-size candle that they each then light with their two small candles. This symbolizes the path of their own individual practice in which they each find their own resolution of these opposites by realizing the perspective of oneness or non-duality. They then each pick up their medium candles and come to the altar in front of one large candle and light that together. This step symbolizes the coming together of their paths, a commitment to support each other and practise together. Through the ceremony there's a recognition of the equal importance of each partner's own individual growth and development, as well as the commitment to helping each other grow through their relationship.

In the following, we'll see two particular and different examples of how a partner became a troublesome Buddha and the lessons they learnt through those experiences. The first can happen (and I might argue *will* happen to some extent) to anyone in a relationship. The second example illustrates how even a catastrophic breakdown of a partnership can become a fertile ground for growth and self-enquiry.

Expressing your feelings as you go along

Since he first met his wife, John observed that often "when she was engrossed in something like reading or browsing on the computer, she wouldn't hear anything I said". In relaxed times, they'd joke about how the things he said would be stored in her internal queueing system to be replayed when she'd finished what she was doing. Occasionally it would be recounted accurately, but most of the time it would end up garbled in some way. In times when he was less relaxed and tolerant, he'd find this habit infuriating. But in the reverse situation, he reflected: "I had the perception that she could say something to me at almost any time and I'd be able to broaden my attention and hear what she was saying."

John realized that what his wife was doing wasn't under her conscious control. "She wasn't choosing to ignore me, her brain simply didn't register what I was saying when she was focusing on something else." He added: "Since I felt like this was something that neither of us could change, I just thought it was my responsibility to accept her behaviour." This went on for a few years, but it didn't put an end to his frustration – it only led to a build-up of unexpressed emotion. John said that in his weaker (and less regulated) moments: "I would express this pent-up emotion through passive aggressive or snide comments that came out some time after the event." This inevitably caused conflict: "I would always come away with a horrible feeling in the pit of my stomach and sense of it being my fault."

After reflecting on what was happening, John decided to start trying to confront his wife at the times when he felt the frustration arising instead of just trying to accept it. He was able to find ways of telling her how he felt when he wasn't being heard ("Putting aside the times that she didn't hear this either..."). "Calmly and honestly describing my feelings at the time I was feeling them felt like a more healthy way of expressing them." As he was able to do this more often, he found the emotional energy wouldn't build up as it had been before and he felt much more at ease. "In turn, my wife began to see how frustrating it was for me when she didn't hear me." Although her behaviour was indeed unconscious, he noticed that "just knowing what effect it had meant that it started to happen less often".

John can now see that when he himself is concentrating hard on something he also occasionally fails to hear, or has a delayed response to something his wife has said. This realization, he said, "has led to a great deal more forgiveness and acceptance of her behaviour".

The lotus blooms in the fire

It's been six years since Anne-Marie ended her fiery marriage – a marriage that she describes as "a crucible that held a karmic bonfire". She said: "My six-foot-five husband came into my life blazing with anger energy. Every few days he would fly into a rage and this formed the primary rhythm of our relationship." She found this extremely difficult to handle and very confusing. As a result, she started questioning everything – looking to see what was happening and applying "an academic level of scrutiny to myself and my relationship".

She couldn't really understand what motivated the outbursts, where the rage was coming from – and even wondered why she was attracted to this man. Although she had come across mildly troublesome people before, nothing had prompted her to look so deeply into herself as this situation. "It was just too big to ignore!"

Anne-Marie initially turned to the medical world for help. "I read everything I could about human dynamics, psychology, suffering, addiction, cultural patterns and family and attachment trauma." She tried a number of psychotherapy modalities before stumbling on a different approach – Zen Buddhism. She found the Zen practices of awareness and compassion, non-judgemental self-enquiry and working one-to-one with a teacher to be the most powerful set of tools for her.

Slowly, through her practice, she "gained a sense of clarity and strength, and, step-by-step, climbed out of the deep hole I'd found myself in." She describes it as "like having a mirror held up to me in stark daylight". In her meetings with her Zen teacher (the free and unconditional meeting of teacher and student is known as *sanzen*), her teacher was able to hold a space in which she could let her rage and anger out safely. "I was able to look at it without it burning everything I touched in the rest of my life." She feels amazingly lucky to have met her teacher and feels deeply indebted to him for all his help.

As her heart opened, she was gradually able to create and hold that space herself where the fire could be fully seen and acknowledged. "As the energy unwound and changed, I started to touch into a deep aching pain." Her husband's behaviour had helped her connect with the denial, suppressed anger and blocked energy that, she discovered, had its roots in her childhood. "My childhood had taught me that violent, aggressive behaviour from others was acceptable. However, it hadn't been safe for me to express any of my own anger." That had taught her to lock her emotions deeply within. She realized that these familiar, violent and aggressive qualities were partly what had initially attracted her to her husband in the first place. "As things opened up further, I saw how his behaviour paralleled the type of things my mother did when she was a child, only writ large." With time she began to see the pattern of unchallenged violence running through the generations of her family.

As a result, for the first time she became able to love her husband for who he was. Being still in the relationship at this point, she saw herself as "a true lotus blooming in the fire" (a traditional Buddhist image that represents our capacity to realize and demonstrate kindness, equanimity and understanding in the midst of suffering). "One night I had a dream of a train reaching the end of the track with a bump, and it was at that point that I knew my relationship was over." She knew she needed to get out of the train and start walking – "I left him immediately. I was getting stronger, feeling more whole and more wise." She went on: "Gradually, through continued practice, I was able to face other aspects of suffering in my life, layer-by-layer, including depression, anxiety and deep levels of intergenerational attachment trauma. During those years, I let so much pour out of my system, sometimes even physically through shaking movements."

Even when they were still together, Anne-Marie had no trouble seeing her husband's innate "energy signature", as she called it – who he was underneath all the effects of being trampled on in his childhood. She knew that nothing was fundamentally broken, bad or irredeemable about him. "He was a flowing, dynamic, interdependent process that was as much part of the universe as everything else. He just couldn't control his rage."

Reflecting now, she acknowledges that she stayed in the relationship partly with the hope that they would be able to heal together. "But in the end he wasn't able to walk that path with me, and for that I feel sad." Although she herself found it possible to make progress while within the relationship, for him it just wasn't the right time. She wrote an email letter to him after they were divorced that was a turning point:

"I thanked him for spending those years with me and for being my teacher. He said he understood."

In Thich Nhat Hanh's analogy of gardening, when you've learnt to selectively water the flowers of love and kindness in your own and your partner's gardens, and in your shared garden, you become a *sangha* (the Buddhist word for community) of two people. Together you can then provide refuge for a third person, and then a fourth, and so on. In this way, your *sangha* will grow. As we'll see in the following chapters, the importance of community in providing us with troublesome situations through which we can learn and grow, and support for helping us through those difficult times, cannot be underestimated.

CHAPTER 10
FAMILY BUDDHAS

The renowned contemporary spiritual teacher, Ram Dass, once said: "If you think you're enlightened, go spend a week with your family."[20] When we return to the family environment that we grew up in, it's all too easy for our hard-earned insights and more developed ways of being to just fly out the window. We easily get sucked back into the negative behavioural patterns that dominated in the years before we left home.

On top of this, family members have an extraordinary ability to press your buttons. Buttons are ideas or subjects that you're particularly sensitive to, and usually have their roots in something that happened when you were young. For example, it drives you crazy when your dad raises an eyebrow at the sight of your hairstyle, or it gets your back up every time your sister makes a reference to "that embarrassing event" from when you were 12. Siblings, in particular, learn early on how to push each other's buttons – often before they recognize they have a button there themselves! As adults, anger and spite can cause us to push another person's buttons on purpose. One of the most destructive patterns that can arise in a relationship is purposeful button pressing. It accomplishes nothing but more pain and unhappiness.

However, when you've developed a habit of awareness and acceptance and spent some time enquiring into yourself, it's a tremendous gift when someone attempts to press one of your buttons – as we'll see in some of the examples below. By doing so they bring into focus an area within you that can still be disturbed. As you become aware of how they're trying to provoke you and the rising signals of your habitual reaction, you have a chance to pause, acknowledge what's happening and make a choice as to how you'll respond next.

Developing and growing as an adult is wonderful, but troublesome situations can arise when those in our family can't see or understand the changes in us and continue to relate to us the way we were in the past. I remember many such situations with my own family and friends. As babies and children, all of us develop some kind of relationship with our parents. But after we grow up and leave home, not everyone makes the final step and develops beyond the child-parent relationship. You might call this entering super-adulthood or true adulthood. For some, their parents are sufficiently wise to allow this transition to happen quite naturally. But for others, they might remain more-or-less stuck in the child role for most of their life, playing out old habits and behavioural patterns with their family and suffering greatly as a result.

In my experience, making this final step is a bit like a crab outgrowing its hard shell. The pressure of feeling confined, limited and stuck in old ways is painful. For some, the motivation or wish to change is strong enough that it creates the energy to drive the growth. Forcing our way out of the shell can sometimes be even more painful – and I know some people that have found it too much and stopped here. But if we do carry on, then finally breaking free of the shell can feel like an enormous relief. Over time, this change can allow all parties to grow and find a new basis for the relationship.

The adjustment process can take a while, and although it can create its own troublesomeness, there's often a sense you're on the right track – it feels wholesome and freeing. We'll see aspects of all these stages in the examples below.

The first two accounts highlight, once again, the importance of noticing the physical sensations that arise around difficult relationships. Franco realized that the difficult interactions he'd been having with his parents had contributed toward a build-up of tension and stiffness in his body. This important insight is a visceral reminder of the interconnectedness of the mind, body and emotions, and how tightness and resistance can manifest in many different ways. Then we'll hear from Ruth, who realized how much she'd become caught up in thoughts, storylines and blame toward her mother. But as she learnt to tune into her body, she found this interrupted her habitual thought patterns and allowed the blame to subside. This then had a dramatic effect on her ability to communicate and relate to her mother.

Letting go of tension and fixed ideas

Franco remembers having a good childhood and was given everything a child could desire. But as he became an adult, every time he spoke to his parents he ended up feeling resentful, upset and misunderstood. "I blamed them for all my issues and felt totally stuck." If they said something that he found challenging, he "would ruminate over it for a long time afterwards and stay stuck, completely unable to let it go". He remembers how his mind would find ways beyond any kind of reasoning to justify all these negative sentiments.

After Franco starting practising Zen and mindfulness, he began to examine his own mind: "I realized how much I'd become stuck in my own deluded world. My fixed ideas, views and opinions had trapped me in a small box, and, at the time, I was completely unable to see beyond it." In this box, he said he "suffered silently and felt separate and alone". His Zen and mindfulness practice gave him a way of allowing that box to open. "Slowly I began to see the wider interconnections I share with my parents, with the environments I've lived in and with the entire universe – an interconnection which encompasses the whole universe, where there is absolutely nothing personal, no gain and no loss." Now, when he interacts with his parents: "I can notice my emotions and underlying negative thoughts emerging but know I no longer need to react to them, there's just the recognition."

In the past year or so, Franco has started practising more yoga and qigong and has realized just how stiff and inflexible his body has become. "Initially, I blamed years of running and cycling, but I've begun to realize that at least part of my stiffness comes from tensing up every time I'm confronted by a troublesome person – little-by-little my body was tightening and closing." Now, every time he speaks to his parents, or when he's in the company of other troublesome-Buddha teachers, he tries to notice the resulting tension arising in his body and accept it as just one of his old habitual patterns. "I can now choose to consciously relax so that my body can start opening up again." Franco knows now that, fundamentally, his body reacts like this because there are still parts of him that perceive the world as separate. Seeing through this fundamental delusion of separateness is at the core of Zen practice. "When we act from the perspective of separateness, then there's something that needs defending and something that can get resentful and hurt."

These days, Franco is grateful for the signals his body sends him that remind him of all his delusions. "I'm thankful for all the troublesome Buddhas who have 'ignited' these signals over the years, especially my parents." He is only now truly able to see and appreciate how they love him, and have always loved him, in their own way.

Inhabiting your own sensations

As Ruth grew up, she harboured a great deal of blame toward her mum for the things she did in her childhood that had shaped her. When Ruth went to university, she deliberately didn't go home during that whole time. She knows her mum was hurt by this, but Ruth wanted as little contact as possible. Ruth's perception of her mum is that "she likes being in control and would take any opportunity to get in my face and try to influence my life". Ruth said of this extended phase of avoidance: "When we spoke on the phone every now and then I was quite unpleasant and rude, telling her she was rambling on and I'd heard it all before, and would often distract myself by doing other things at the same time." She found these encounters would physically wind her up, making her angry. These habitual responses, she remembers, would play out whenever they made contact.

Some years later when Ruth started practising Zen, she started to look at the nature of her suffering. "I'd been seeing my problems with my mother purely intellectually in the world of concepts and thoughts." As she learnt how to become aware of her physical feelings without the judgement of thoughts, she was able to move away from the blaming. "The practice of awareness interrupted my habitual reactions and provided a space – not a remote, cold space, but a personal nourishing space – where I could start seeing the miasma of stuff that was arising around my suffering." This enquiry made her shut up and actually listen to, for example, "the prickly feeling in my gut that I just didn't want to be there". With time, she said, "I became acutely aware of a whole variety of uncomfortable sensations in my heart and belly".

Contact with her mum continued to bring up frustration and annoyance, but she now noticed a new thought – "that I was being un-Buddhist in the way I resented and avoided her". Putting that aside as essentially another judgement, she knew her true work was in continuing to face her difficult feelings. "My desire to leave the painful place I was in and let go of my suffering provided the motivation to keep my practice going." She began to recognize some of the boundaries and walls that she'd constructed around her feelings and, as she learnt about trauma and started practising yoga, focused on working with her stuff on a physical level.

"I really, really struggled with this process; it was a rocky and difficult time in my life. As I learnt to allow and actually inhabit my own sensations more deeply, I found that instead of reacting negatively and moving away I could actually begin moving toward my mother. My harsh responses began to soften and I found more kindness and compassion." She experimented with other ways of communicating with her mum that made for more manageable yet meaningful interactions, like text messaging and sending physical postcards.

Ruth decided to regard phone calls with her mum as a time to practise being totally present. "When scheduling a call, I would make sure I had adequate time, put aside any distractions and give my mum my full attention as she chatted away." She realized that communicating with her mum may always be difficult, but as a result of her work has noticed some real changes. "My mum recently commented on how nice I am to her these days." Ruth has noticed her mum has started to reciprocate that niceness.

Not long ago on a Zen retreat, the relationship shifted to a whole new level. "During my meditation practice I was able to see my mum's original form, her true state, without all the accumulations of suffering that had arisen from her upbringing and the restraints she'd had during her life." After this shift, Ruth found a completely natural compassion for her mum arising. "The effort and trying that had been there before was no longer needed. I began seeing my mum as herself, recognizing her innate humour. I was able to relax into chatting normally."

During her precepts ceremony a few years ago for formally committing to the Buddhist path, Ruth remembered the moment when she was asked to make a bow to her parents. "I did the action at the time but didn't really mean it." More recently, she has had an overwhelming desire to genuinely bow to her parents. "So I asked my teacher if I could make the bow again in front of him, and this time I truly meant it."

In the next account, we'll see how the difficulties in Henry's relationship with his parents came from seeking approval for something he was doing, and not finding it. As a result he felt he had to lie and things turned uncomfortable. Through his introspection, he realized that the difficulties he was having with his parents were really reflecting his own insecurities about how he saw himself and who he wanted to be.

Getting to the point where there's no such thing as Zen

Henry has practised Zen for ten years, since he was 25. For a long time, he felt the need for his spirituality to be seen and acknowledged – especially by his parents. "My parents always looked at my interest in Zen with worry and confusion. They'd never want to talk about it and most of the time would actively avoid the subject." His parents were atheists and he thought they were probably prejudiced against any religion or spiritual practice. "The fact that I couldn't talk about it made it into a real 'thing' and highlighted the fact that we weren't relating – even though I wanted to." As a result, Henry found himself lying to his parents about what he was doing, saying that he was working instead of actually being on a retreat, creating a clear disconnect between what he was saying and how he was.

When they did manage to talk about it, it would be uncomfortable. "They might say one little thing that really niggled me, like a comment about meditation seeming a bit selfish, and it would really bother me for ages." He got annoyed at being niggled because, he thought, "Zen practice is supposed to bring peace". He went on: "It seemed to me this brought out the complete hypocrisy of the thing." Doubts abounded. What also upset him was why he got so frustrated by what his parents said when one part of him actually agreed. "Why would it flag up in me if I didn't believe it myself at some level?"

Henry can see now that all of this was good grist for the mill of his practice. Gradually he realized it wasn't necessarily about them, but more about his own attitudes and beliefs. "I wasn't relating to life very well. I realized there had to be something wrong with the way I was seeing things."

He reflected on how his parents "regularly challenged me on how I saw Zen and how I related to it – just through being who they were". A major shift happened after one such challenge. "After I'd responded to my mum with something like 'I just want to talk about Zen', my mum said 'you know, probably in the future, Zen will become just who you are and you won't have to talk about it any more'." Henry remembers finding that surprisingly insightful. "That really hit the nail on the head, because I knew I wanted it to become a completely integrated part of who I am, not something special or different."

When I asked him whether he'd reached the point where there's "no such thing as Zen", he said "I'm getting there…!" He added: "It feels less and less like something that could be lost or even defined. I now understand it on a much more experiential level, where I didn't so much before." He finds he no longer talks so much about it with his parents. "I don't try to convince them or explain it like I used to. They see me meditating but don't question it." He's told them that if they get worried about what Zen is doing to him, "Just pay attention to how I am – if I'm becoming a better, nicer person, then it's going okay!" So far they haven't complained.

The next two examples centre on the anguish of wanting things to be a certain way when they just aren't or can't be. In the first, Clive describes how he felt like he could only be happy if he managed to heal his relationship with his parents, but encountered strong resistance when he tried discussing his problems with them. Then I describe from my own life how I wanted my mum to do things she just wasn't capable of. We'll see how Clive and I gradually came to terms with who our parents were and accepted our respective situations. In my example, I found I had to go through a grieving process for the loss of the person I wished for. In both examples, the result of this acceptance was an increased sense of freedom and ease. Once we acknowledged that we didn't have the power to change our parents, it was similarly important for us to find ways of making the relationship work around the areas of difficulty. These techniques made it possible for us to enjoy our time together with our parents while minimizing the suffering.

Awareness and acceptance of yourself as you are now

Clive was born the youngest of four kids and, as he grew up, felt "the least consequential in the group". From his present-day, grown-up perspective, he recognizes: "Through my family situation, I must have learnt at an early age to bury my feelings and become someone different. As I became an adult and went to university I wished someone could just see through my mask and hear what I wasn't able to say." During these years, he harboured a great bitterness and resentment toward his parents and felt totally unseen and lonely.

With the help of a psychotherapist, Clive began recognizing the childhood roots of his suffering and pain. Despite the pain, he derived a sense of relief from simply identifying the issues that he was suffering from. "I reached a stage where I felt I could only be happy if I healed my relationship with my parents – which put me in a kind of dependency on them." With a desperate yearning to heal, he went through a period of contacting them and trying to discuss his feelings with them. However, in response, he encountered a distinct unwillingness from his parents to examine or discuss their past behaviour and gradually felt "it wasn't healthy for me to continue in this direction".

The real game changer came when he realized that to heal he didn't need to address the whys and wherefores of what had happened when he was a child. "The healing could happen through awareness and acceptance of myself as I am now, without the involvement of my parents at all." Initially with the help of his therapist, then later through the practice of mindfulness and Zen, he explored what it was like to feel the pain physically, in his body, without engaging with the associated thoughts and storylines.

Over time, he became increasingly confident in putting into practice the techniques of awareness, acceptance and non-judgement. Gradually he even began to enjoy a sense of freedom within himself. "In stark contrast to the premeditated, censored or vetted conversations I'd always had with my parents in the past, I found I was able to speak more freely and easily with them."

Reflecting back, the changes in Clive's relationship with his parents have been slow and sometimes difficult to see. "But certainly the peaks and valleys have gradually softened." On a practical level: "I found that withdrawing to a quiet place for 30–60 minutes both before and after meeting with them has been incredibly helpful." He would dedicate this time to becoming aware of the physical effects of the suffering that arose from being with his parents. He gave those sensations the space to just be there. "It was like creating a container around these meetings in order to give myself a chance to mop up any left-over suffering before re-entering my normal life." Later, he also started to introduce additional small spaces during the day, particularly around difficult interactions, to give himself a chance to really tune into his feelings, allow them to be and let things settle. "While I'd always hated Christmases with my parents, by using these techniques I found I actually started to enjoy them a little."

A major shift came when he recognized that the pain he was feeling wasn't just personal or self-centred, but had a kind of impersonal or collective nature. "My view opened up from just seeing myself and my own pain, to something much broader

– the interconnected suffering of the whole world. Suddenly things became simpler and I found a deep welling up of compassion." A compassion that transcended himself and his parents, going far beyond the individual.

Although he's noticed a growing contentment in his relationship with his parents, they continue to be his teachers. "It's just the lessons they teach seem much more doable!" He still gets many bodily reactions whenever he's with them but has learnt how to work with them more skilfully. "Carving out time and really acknowledging and accepting all that I'm feeling takes effort and discipline, and a strong intention to stay grounded." But over time his skills and experience with the practices have grown, and so has his confidence and trust in them. "It's much easier to step out of a reactive mindset into a more settled, expansive one where I can avoid getting involved in the storylines that swirl around." He's noticed himself generally feeling more steady and peaceful, and more able to be himself and at ease in interactions.

Wanting my mum to be like a normal mum

As I mentioned earlier, when I was 13 my mum and stepdad were involved in a car accident. My stepdad was killed and my mum ended up having both her legs and one arm amputated. As a result I wasn't given much of a chance to be a teenager. Mum did her best to look after me and my sister, but was limited in what she could do. Much of my emotional energy and attention was devoted toward helping mum live her life as well as navigating the day-to-day challenges of getting to school and back. When I started psychotherapy and Zen practice in my mid-20s, I began to realize that I had developed a desperate wish for her to be like a normal mum. At first I recognized only a general frustration. Over time I began to see more specifically that I craved physical touch from her (she was never a naturally tactile person and her disability – particularly the wheelchair – prevented this even more). I wanted her to be able to do stuff with me, come and visit me at university, be more emotionally available and have more head-space. It didn't matter how much I intellectually understood why she wasn't able to give me what I wanted; I still wanted it.

I also wished for her to participate in life as fully as possible – to enjoy things as much as we did. On different occasions my sister and I both tried to get her to come to the theatre, go to the beach, come camping or go for long walks in the forest – all of which were technically possible but difficult for her. Even some things that seemed fairly straightforward – like going to a suitably adapted theatre – were so stressful for her that the anxiety would overwhelm any pleasure she would derive from it such that, for her, the overall experience would be negative.

It took her a long time to accept what she could and couldn't do – but I think it took my sister and me longer. Once I was able to acknowledge what I sought (and couldn't get) from the relationship, things slowly began to soften. The process of acceptance took many years and was like grieving for the loss of the person I wanted her to be. I gradually realized that I would have to find the things I looked for from her somewhere else.

In time, our relationship reached a point that was comfortable and enjoyable. I learnt to negotiate our time together so that we generally avoided the most troublesome and intractable issues. I would limit my visits to a few days at most, and do my best not to expect anything from her. That meant I really appreciated it when she did make the effort – like spending a few hundred pounds on hiring a wheelchair-adapted taxi to come and attend my graduation ceremony (despite the huge stress it would have caused her), or making a special effort when my wife came one Christmas.

This whole process of learning to let go of who I wanted her to be and accepting who she was, was a huge lesson for me in how wanting and wishing creates suffering. Ultimately, I saw how my idea of who I wanted her to be was preventing me from seeing her as she really was, and it was just acting to get in the way of our relationship.

That's not to say I didn't continue to struggle with wanting what she couldn't give right up to the day she died. I had really hoped she'd be willing to spend Christmas with my wife's family sometime. She resisted, knowing that the difficulties with logistics and finding toilets would make it stressful. But I was aware there was a part of me that still wanted it.

So far we've heard accounts of people who had troublesome relationships with parents. The following two examples centre on troublesome siblings. Michelle's example once again illustrates the importance of recognizing when we become caught up in thoughts and storylines – about who said what, why they said what they did and reasoning out what we should do next – and instead switch our attention to the body and our sensations. It's only when we're able to tune into our body that we can hope to express honestly what we're feeling. Then we'll hear from Paul and the saga that ensued after his father's death. Paul discovered how important it was to acknowledge that each of his siblings and relations had a different perspective and to let go of the multifarious storylines, narratives and opinions about who was right. He ultimately found he needed to just accept what had transpired, however painful and confusing.

Manipulating a troublesome person

Michelle has always found her younger sister incredibly irritating. "She would regularly and intentionally push my buttons and rattle my cage just to try and get a rise out of me." Michelle has found her Zen practice helpful in dealing with her sister's button-pushing. However, while they were recently communicating about something rather mundane, the energy of their conversation slowly rose: "I felt my sister was provoking me, angling for a fight. Eventually I lost it and really let rip. I sent her a stinking text message, but as soon as I pressed send, I came back to my senses." She recognized: "I'd become completely caught up in my head – wrapped up in thoughts about how difficult my sister was being and reacting to them out of habit."

She realized she'd been trying to "think out" the best way to deal with her and manipulate the situation instead of honestly and freshly expressing her feelings as they arose. Michelle told me: "This situation reminded me that it takes quite some strength to stay present, authentic and truthful as the energy of a troublesome interaction rises. It also takes time to feel out and learn different strategies for diffusing the situation within yourself and within the interaction – especially when there are powerful old habits at play."

A huge rift in the family

A few years ago Paul's dad died. During the period immediately before and after his death, his sister Joan did a variety of things that Paul found extremely troublesome. First, she missed their brother's wedding to visit their poorly dad, and while she was there Paul found it odd and difficult that she didn't send any updates on his condition (as he would have wanted to do). She then announced that, when the time came, she wouldn't be going to the funeral.

As Paul received news that his father was nearing the end, he jumped on the first train. "During the journey, I got a call from Joan questioning me as to why I was going. I found this question and her behaviour at the time challenging. Then I got a message saying Joan had changed her mind and would now be flying over to be there too." In the midst of it all, Paul was grateful that, at the moment of his death, all four siblings ended up at his father's bedside.

Later that evening there were arguments in which, contrary to previous occasions, Joan sided with Paul's stepmother, Jenny. As they were all leaving, a cousin took all the siblings aside and told them that Jenny had had their dad's will changed not long before he died and now everything was left to her.

Paul said: "I felt fine about this, since I didn't stand to inherit much anyway." But Joan was now adamant that wasn't what their dad wanted. She told them that their dad had told her that he wanted to leave everything to the grandchildren. Feeling confused and hurt, Paul considered with his siblings that they may need to challenge the new will, so they agreed that he would make some initial enquiries with solicitors in the area on behalf of the family. In the next couple of months he began doing so, but he was surprised to hear that many of the solicitors had already spoken with Joan over the past few weeks. Happy that they were going to challenge the new will, Joan now claimed that their dad had promised her that she was to inherit everything.

Paul admitted that the acts of deceptions and mistrust from Joan caused a huge rift in the family. For about a year Paul struggled with how to process it all. He wondered what to do and whether he could let her get away with it. Once the apparent deception came to light, Joan stopped talking to any of the other siblings, and Paul entered into a long period of great difficulty in his personal life.

In time, Paul got more seriously into meditation and Zen practice. He started to try and work out his own feelings and examine the various different perceptions of each family member. "After initially blaming Joan I saw that her actions weren't directed at me specifically. It's just that she has a very different view." This, he sees, was the first step he took toward a wiser outlook – realizing that other people have their own perspectives. Around that time, Paul was struck by a line from a book by the contemporary Zen master Thich Nhat Hanh, saying you can't love someone if you don't truly know them. So Paul wrote to Joan: "In the letter I expressed my feeling of loss for a sister, that I wished things had been different and that it was hard to understand what she did." He asked to meet with her to hear her side of the story. Joan agreed to meet for a coffee.

During the meeting Paul said: "I was able to embody the skills and practices of Zen and talk about my feelings without a sense of judgement for Joan's actions." Paul sees this as his second step to a more wise approach – to listen. However, Joan avoided his questions and redirected the conversation away from what had happened. As they parted, Paul was disappointed. "In the following few years, I struggled with how to deal with all the shoulds – like she's my sister so I should love her, or I should try harder."

Gradually he realized he'd met her with a judgemental attitude; that if what she said and how she explained herself was good enough, then he might forgive her. "If I have to understand her before I can forgive her, then the forgiveness is conditional." Paul didn't want to spend his life waiting for an explanation of her actions or to harbour any more negative feelings toward her. "So I forgave her, and that allowed me to start being able to simply wish her well."

Now he appreciates that their relationship can't change "without her making some movement toward accepting and taking responsibility for her actions". He's realized that "how she behaves when we do have communication isn't helpful and often creates more difficulty and pain". So Paul has also been working on letting go of his desire to have a different relationship. "It's hard when you want someone to be happier than they will allow themselves to be."

To Paul it seems Joan has remained stuck in an attitude of lack – full of fear and the need to cling to stuff. He knows she's not a terrible person and no less a human than anyone else. In fact, he said: "I very much recognize that mindset of lack and fear in myself. It's just that she's learnt certain behaviours from her particular set of life circumstances that have played out in our family." It's now been over ten years since his dad died, and in that time Paul has found the third step to a wiser approach: "Letting go of all the storylines, wishes and wants, and just accepting things for what they are."

The last four examples in this chapter centre on children (who, let's face it, are troublesome Buddhas most of the time!). One of the things they teach us is how to be present. Children – especially young children – live in the present moment. They don't worry about the future just as much as they don't worry about anything that's not right in front of them at that moment. In that sense, they're fantastic little Zen masters, embodying a true "beginner's mind" in everything they do (Shunryu Suzuki talked about this in his book *Zen Mind, Beginner's Mind*). But that doesn't stop them from being frustrating, difficult, incomprehensible or downright mischievous. As they grow older it can seem sometimes like their troublesomeness only increases. But they can continue to teach us deep lessons in a multitude of ways – showing us how to find patience, humility, trust and what it is to love unconditionally.

First, off, we'll hear how a conflict with Sarah's husband over a Christmas gift for one of their children provided her with the opportunity to reflect deeply on her beliefs and attitudes. Then we'll hear from Antonio. As is increasingly the case these days, one of his grown-up children came back to live in the family home, and in doing so created a wonderfully troublesome opportunity for growth and learning for him. In both examples, it was through acknowledging and accepting the uncomfortable physical responses and associated mental whirlwinds that some important insights could arise around their parenting responsibilities and what it means to let go of wanting things to go a certain way.

The possibility that you might be wrong

Since Sarah started meditating and practising Zen, she's noticed how hard and fixed her attitudes had become, particularly with respect to her husband and their parenting responsibilities.

"As we started to set boundaries and rules for our growing children, I found that the differences between my husband's childhood and mine started to cause friction. He came from a conservative, strict and quite religious family with a strong sense of duty, whereas my family was liberal, atheist and quite relaxed in terms of rules." She became aware that the behavioural patterns she'd experienced as a child were now coming out through her parenting.

At first, both of them took a definite "I'm right, you're wrong" stance and reacted strongly in response to each other's attitudes. "Later, as I began to meditate and look into myself, I started to consider the possibility that I might not be right in every circumstance." One instance stands out in particular, when she and her husband had a major disagreement over a Christmas gift they'd bought for one of their children. "As I was sitting alone in the car meditating, it dawned on me that I was only 95 per cent certain of being right. As I sat with the possibility of being wrong, I did my best not to react but just observe the plethora of responses in my body." She admitted that "in this case, I had been wrong".

After facing criticism or after having her opinions or beliefs challenged, Sarah confessed that her normal pattern was to sulk. "With time, I saw how unproductive and self-indulgent this was." Looking back, it makes her laugh to remember how she used to do this so often.

She remembers that "a major change came when I realized that my thoughts aren't necessarily the truth". Prior to this she had just believed her thoughts without question. Sarah finds it extraordinary that she got so far in life without realizing this. Before mindfulness and Zen, her only encounter with trying to understand her mind was in her early 20s when, after a particularly stressful time, she took up a work counselling scheme. She said the extent of what she learnt was to punch a cushion when she felt frustrated.

She told me: "Negative thoughts are often generated as the result of habitual patterns and beliefs; they're the root of so many of our anxieties." She also saw how many of her and her husband's disagreements were being fuelled by these kinds of habitual thoughts. "It was a mind-blowing discovery!" She went on: "Since then, I've tried to make it part of my practice to try and catch myself as my thoughts and perceptions start leading to a hardening of my stance." She said she tries to acknowledge, allow and accept those feelings and attitudes, and see them as just one view "that may very well be wrong". She realized: "There's more to it than just being right!"

The great wall of blank

As children grow up and become adults, the nature of the parental relationship changes. Antonio's children are all in their 20s. After having left home to study at university, his youngest, Sebastian, moved back – and has since become one of Antonio's most prominent troublesome teachers.

No matter how much Antonio and his wife try, "It seems at this point in his life, Sebastian just isn't interested in connecting and engaging with us on any level beyond the purely practical." Antonio went on: "I've got emotions and experiences that I want to share with Sebastian, but all I get is 'the great wall of blank'." As parents, not being able to get a sense of Sebastian's emotional state worries them. "I don't know whether we should have a genuine concern or if it's just his hormones – or whether he's just reacting against having to live with us again. He has friends and is good with other people – just not with us." Just about the only time Sebastian will engage is when he pulls one of them up for making some half-thought-through comment he doesn't agree with. Antonio wonders whether he just needs to re-calibrate his expectations – "After all, the nature of a parent's relationship with their child is that it continually changes as years go by, and things can easily become stuck (on both sides) without that regular re-calibration." He told me that what gives him and his wife some reassurance and solace is that during this period they can at least offer him shelter, good food and a comfortable environment to live in.

Through his meditation practice, Antonio has increasingly begun to notice the physical response to being regularly confronted by Sebastian's "testy behaviour" – in the form of muscular tension and a rising sense of heat. "I've been surprised to discover the number of narratives and stories I've been carrying about how I see myself and my family." He's noticed his tendencies to want to fix his children's problems and prevent them from making the mistakes that he made. But, he said: "I've increasingly been able to put these wants aside and create space for my children to grow, make mistakes and be themselves." He knows he must let go. "I have to trust that through our years of parenting, we have inculcated in our children a healthy set of values and attitudes from which they can make their own decisions." He added: "But doing that, while frequently having to wash Sebastian's smelly socks, has been challenging!"

Buddha-nature has manifested clearly for Antonio through his family. "The birth of Sebastian all those years ago jolted me into an immediate sense of connection with my own father and grandfathers." Over the years, this has opened up into a much broader, intergenerational view on life. "For me, it's been a process of accepting the chaotic, unpredictable nature of family life and finding a deep value in its pure 'is-ness'. It seems that it was just through being myself and allowing the family to be itself that many of the values I inherited from my parents, and their parents before that, have been passed down to Sebastian and our other children." This natural, almost inevitable flow of connection gives Antonio a feeling of oneness with them and his family up and down through the generations, and indeed with the whole universe. "With this comes a definite sense of something that goes beyond life and death."

This next account describes Lizzy's arduous relationship with her son, beginning from the day he was born, and the challenges she's faced as he has grown up. Driven by her deep motherly love, she stuck with him through thick and thin. Through this journey, her son has taught her a number of important lessons in parenting, including how important it is to look after herself in order to stay strong and how to deal with uncertainty. Her honest willingness to look within has allowed her to uncover a number of insights that have dramatically changed the course of their lives.

Uncovering the Buddha light

Lizzy had her first child when she was quite young. It was a painful and traumatic birth and afterwards she found it extremely difficult to bond with the little baby boy. "I just didn't get that elated mother feeling." Baby Olly was lively and, as she put it, "high-spirited (naughty!) and clearly intelligent" but he screamed a lot and was often ill. Throughout his toddler years, he ended up in and out of hospital with kidney problems.

Since Olly's father wasn't present and Lizzy lived far from her family and friends, she felt isolated and lonely. "I recognized the signs of depression, but was frightened that if I was officially diagnosed and had to go into hospital, Olly would be taken away from me. So I self-medicated with antidepressants." However, these made her feel numb and robotic, which compounded her fear that she was being a bad mum. "For years I struggled to get a good night's sleep and felt that all Olly's problems were my fault."

At age nine, it was found that Olly's liver was producing toxins that had been making him ill. This diagnosis and subsequent treatment took a huge weight off Lizzy's mind, but by that point many wheels had already been set in motion. "He continued to be badly behaved and was a real handful at home." Since his dad didn't want anything to do with him, she thought, it was likely Olly felt abandoned. "He stood out like a sore thumb at school because of his behaviour, always being mischievous and getting into crazy scrapes." She remembers feeling just too tired to engage with teachers, and, as a result, guilty that she didn't fight his corner hard enough.

Olly became a troubled teenager, lying, stealing and continuing to get into trouble. Although Lizzy only found out much later, he started experimenting with drugs around the age of 13. "I had an aching love for him, but no clue really how to help him." Their relationship took on a push-pull dynamic, and although she loved him, she often found it difficult to actually like him. "Looking back, I see myself now as a bit naïve, feeling dazed and confused and not really knowing anything about the drug scene."

Olly left home at 17 and became homeless. Lizzy was desperately worried about him but again didn't really know how to help. "Sometimes, I was able to take him food, offer him some money or collect him from hospital, but other times I wouldn't actually want to go near him because it was scary." He couldn't hold down a job, and lied and manipulated people due to his drug dependency. "I fell into a debilitating state of self-centred victimhood, desperately asking 'why me?' and 'why my son?'" Olly's father told her she should ignore him and that he wasn't worth her attention, "but I simply couldn't do that", she said.

Lizzy began practising Zen when Olly was 20. To begin with, she found any meditation practices that involved open awareness were too difficult: "My attention would be overtaken by a sickening worry about Olly that frequently developed into catastrophizing thoughts." In order to give her overactive mind something more concrete and positive to focus on she began visualizing Olly flooded by light and surrounded by others who loved him. One day, after finishing a run along Hadrian's Wall, she was browsing in a shop and a book on Buddhism literally fell on her head. She said: "I remember reading something like, 'Your Buddha light is within, wrapped up inside a bundle of filthy rags. Your job is to uncover the rags from this jewel of Buddha-nature'. I recognized Olly immediately, except it was worse than rags – it was heaps of shit." His Buddha light was in there somewhere, she knew it was. She saw it as her job to dig it out and help it shine.

Uncovering Olly's Buddha light has turned out to be a journey of her own self-discovery and growth. Reflecting back, she said: "Olly has taught me that getting angry and shouting just doesn't work, and the importance of finding a moment to pause and reframe my heightened emotions before responding." She went on to say: "He's taught me the importance of taking care of myself so that I can be strong and grounded for him when needed." This was a long and tough lesson, she reflected, since he'd always been so completely the centre of her anxious attention that even the thought of looking after herself in any way would irritate her. "He's taught me how to stay with uncertainty – knowing that uncertainty is sometimes the best place to be. And he's taught me how to grow out of my victim mindset and to ask for help without feeling ashamed." She marvels that Olly's reach has been a lot further than he would ever imagine.

Most recently, Lizzy has learnt the profound value of listening with a non-judgemental presence – resisting the temptation to try and fix things or give advice, in fact not even thinking about it – only offering the gift of presence. "When I've been able to listen to Olly in this way, I can see that he responds differently and has even said he can find more clarity and make better decisions. In my view, this kind of attentive, open-minded listening is the only way to really help anyone." Whereas before she'd be impatient and dismissive of others' suffering, realizing the interconnected Buddha-nature in all things has allowed her to find a deep empathetic love and a wish for all beings to be free from suffering. Lizzy considers that she had always underestimated Olly's determination, intelligence and capacity for kindness. "When he was using lots of drugs he wasn't kind, but that wasn't really him." Thinking of this Buddha-nature jewel hidden under the layers of his behaviour – a nature, she remarked, "that she shares with him, and with all other beings" – "It has taught me what it means to love unconditionally."

This journey has helped Lizzy develop a trust in the universe, knowing that answers will always appear when she truly listens.

She now feels so grateful for Olly and all the lessons he's taught her. Although she sees him only now and then when he reaches out, she recognizes his little Buddha light beginning to emerge. He's less angry and more appreciative that the world also has nice people and good experiences to have. "I'm so proud of him."

I'd like to end this chapter on a lighter note, and share with you this final example from Cheryl. In it, Cheryl describes how her son taught her the value of playfulness and how you're never too busy to stop and have a laugh.

The joy of being silly

Cheryl had been a busy mum as her children grew up, working part-time while her husband was away a lot. When her youngest son was in his mid-teens, he discovered a regular video series on the internet featuring silly and funny clips. When he started asking Cheryl to watch them with him, she remembers: "I was impatient and irritated as I'd invariably be making dinner or busy doing something else around the house."

Despite her resistance he kept badgering her. "I started watching the clips for a few minutes at a time and realized that he was just wanting to spend some relaxed time with me. My initially dismissive attitude gradually softened and, with time, I began to realize the value of these moments of shared fun and laughter." She went on: "We'd end up having a really good laugh and would find the funniest clip and watch it over and over." And as the two of them did that more often, that encouraged the rest of her family to join in.

This situation highlighted to Cheryl the prevalence of her "I'm too busy" thoughts and the resistance she'd developed to doing something frivolous and playful. "Slowly I started to appreciate my teenage boy's general silliness – which I'd seen for long time as just irritating – as the natural behaviour of a happy, playful child just being themselves." She told me she's grateful to them for showing her that. "I'm also grateful to be shown how, as a tired, stressed and busy parent, I'd just forgotten how to be silly and playful." In the years afterwards, she remembers it being much easier to share those funny, silly moments with her children as they engaged with her more often.

CHAPTER 11
TEACHER BUDDHAS

Teachers and role models are people we look up to, aspire to be like, try to emulate and learn from. And, as in all relationships, there's a possibility that one (or many) of them could become a troublesome Buddha. However, in contrast to people in other arenas, we assume that our teachers are in some way ahead of us on the path of life and have something useful to teach us. This means our relationships with them (and hence our troubles with them) can be of a slightly different nature to those that we've discussed so far.

We all look up to certain people at various times – whether they're at a distance (like celebrities) or in close proximity (like our parents, teachers or other community members). Since we're unlikely to develop a troublesome relationship with a celebrity we've never met, I'd like to focus the rest of this chapter on our relationship with teachers and mentors – and, in particular, spiritual teachers.

Since time immemorial, the role of a teacher has been recognized as key to the process of learning, but to learn from them we must first trust them. In Buddhism, for example, an initial level of trust in a teacher (sometimes called faith) is encouraged by them being recognized as part of a lineage with a direct line of succession from the Buddha. As our personal relationship with them develops, of course our level of trust deepens and shifts onto its own footing.

In mindfulness and Zen, it is hard to become aware of the gamut of our experience, including all our impulsive wishes, aversions and delusive ideas. Facing ourselves is difficult – and at times can be deeply uncomfortable. Accepting this trust, then, the teacher's role is to urge their students to go beyond where they might go just by themselves. Eventually, a good teacher will encourage a student to internalize that trust and develop a strong belief in themselves.

Because of the intimacy involved in any student–teacher relationship, it's an obvious dynamic in which childhood issues can play out. For example, a student might transfer some of the troublesome nature of their relationship with their parents onto the teacher. A common situation is when the student is looking to their teacher as a replacement parent. Most often this happens totally unconsciously (at least to begin with). In my case, since my father turned out to be abusive and my stepfather was killed when I was 13, I missed a strong father-figure through most of my childhood and adolescence. I'm certain I was (at least to some extent) attracted to my Zen teacher because I was yearning for a nurturing father-figure. Over the years I've noticed wanting to be his favourite or best student, I've asked him for advice about romantic relationships and life decisions and I've found myself repeatedly looking to him for validation and acceptance. I now know these are typical things that students look for in a teacher who is taking the place of a parent. A student in this position might, on one hand, feel disappointed and let down if they don't find the things they're craving. On the other hand, if the teacher (knowingly or unknowingly) fulfils what the student is craving, then the pattern just continues and nothing gets resolved. Either way, sooner or later the teacher will become a troublesome person in the student's eyes. It's even possible that students who don't get what they crave from their teacher may start to see them in such a troublesome light that they end up taking some kind of "revenge" on them. However, in the hands of a sufficiently skilled, conscious and responsible teacher, what might start off as a re-run of a child-parent dynamic can gradually evolve into something more mature as the student's suffering is brought non-judgementally into the light and let go.

Attachment theory, as described in chapter 3, provides a helpful context in which we can understand how some of our unresolved "stuff" from childhood might end up arising in our intimate adult relationships. If you remember, the theory proposes that an infant creates a secure attachment pattern when their caregivers were available and responsive to their needs and sufficiently reliable in that offering. However, if an infant comes to believe their need for love won't be met reliably, they may learn to withdraw or close down. As this child grows up, they might end up leaning toward the aversion-avoidance pattern. They may deny the importance of loved ones in their life and portray themselves as fiercely independent. As a result they may have difficulty in trusting others – including any kind of authority figure like a teacher. Alternatively, a child may become overly demanding and, as an adult, could find themselves in the craving-desire pattern. People in this pattern often try to hold on to their loved ones for dear life, and as a result they could be drawn to authority figures like teachers. If a child's caregiver was sometimes loving and present but sometimes absent, then the child might conclude that the absent times were their fault. As a result, as they grow up they may constantly doubt themselves and their relationships, including that with their teachers – and thus have difficulty trusting their teachers.

With that in mind, let's explore two particular issues that can crop up in our relationship with a teacher (or role model) that relate to things we may have lacked as a child: wanting them to be perfect and having trouble with authority.

Wanting them to be perfect

When we come into contact with someone we aspire to or want to learn from, it's completely natural to find ourselves putting them on a pedestal, idealizing or even idolizing them. If we're not careful, we can make them into exalted Buddhas a little too quickly. A similar thing often happens at the beginning of a romantic relationship. We perceive the other as "perfect" – when evidently they're not. The problem here stems from seeing a changing, dynamic and fallible *process* (the person) as a fixed *thing* or object. By doing that we get stuck. Inevitably our fantasy will one day clash with reality and we will suffer (sometimes a great deal) as a result.

Buddhist teachers through the centuries have been all too aware of this human fallacy (and potential major blockage on the path to awakening) and have developed a number of ways of dealing with it. In Tibetan Buddhism, the approach is to encourage the student to actually put their teacher on a pedestal – but do it with their eyes open. They are often asked to visualize their teacher as a fully enlightened Buddha and present them offerings and dedications. This is to help students see them as an ideal to aspire to and hence provide motivation for practice. In response, Tibetan Buddhist teachers will purposefully remain aloof, maintaining a sense of "professional distance" from their students. Ideally the student never gets to see their foibles and thus their perception of them can never be shattered. As a result, Tibetan Buddhists have a saying: "Always keep at least two valleys between yourself and your teacher."

The approach taken in Zen is slightly different. Students, in my experience, are not asked to imagine their teacher as any kind of deity, but to see and relate to them as ordinary humans. Knowing that some students will regardless always put them on a pedestal, many Zen teachers will go to pains to demonstrate their human fallibility. My Zen teacher, Daizan Roshi (*roshi* being the Japanese for "old teacher" and an honorific given to a Zen master), remembers his Japanese teacher, Shinzan Miyamae Roshi, never giving anyone a chance to create a perfect fantasy version of him.

Madly, deeply real

By the time Daizan came to study with Shinzan Roshi in Japan, he had already been a monk in the UK for 15 years. Over the six years that they lived together, Shinzan became an incredibly troublesome Buddha for him. "From the outset I could see that Shinzan was a disaster area on so many levels – just being around him was ongoing chaos. He was bad with money and was always being ripped off. He would make mad, hopeless decisions, and have crazy ideas on a regular basis. I literally didn't know what was going to happen next." Daizan even remembers an occasion when a visitor pulled a knife on one of the monks. In a sense, Shinzan had created a community of troublesome Buddhas. "He actively recruited them from all over the country! Shinzan would never ask the individuals to change – he would always say 'it's okay, it's alright'. He left you with no choice but to face the situation and accept it (or leave). Being around him was exhausting."

At the same time Daizan recognized something deeply real in Shinzan. "There was absolutely no pretence – everything was just the way it was. It was obvious that Shinzan was touching and living something true, and it was an amazing opportunity to be around him." He said that living with him was a process of learning to see both dimensions at once – the craziness and the deep truth. "By staying with it, I learned a lot. We showed each other those dark places in our being that still needed to come into the light – to be seen and accepted. I gained a deep grounding in what was important – how you deal with difficulties and challenges as they arise, moment-to-moment, with authenticity."

Daizan went on: "Shinzan Roshi never allowed people to put him into a false position – to make him into a big daddy or the solution to all their problems." Partly this was through his maddening behaviour, and partly through, on occasion, "being unbelievably rude". Daizan recalled: "I never got the sense he was manipulating circumstances, though – he was just very natural."

"The lessons were intense and came at a fast pace, and with this approach there were casualties. The crazy chaos was part and parcel of being with Shinzan Roshi. You either got the learning or drowned (left)." Daizan likened his experience to being on a rowboat, with Shinzan pulling the oars and making a complete hash of it. "You could either moan or pick up another set of oars and help. Shinzan provided an amazing opportunity in which you could actually do that – to step up." Daizan said he was sure that's what he was looking for in his students. "Over the years as I stepped up more and more, Shinzan made more space for that to happen. It was an unbelievable privilege to have that time with him."

These days, Daizan also has no qualms about admitting his own various inadequacies. With this approach, he told me, the people who are looking for a faultless guru will be disappointed and will perhaps go off somewhere else. But personally I myself have found (and I think many others also find) that his obvious imperfections make him far more approachable. Like many of us, he often spills the milk when pouring it into tea (sometimes all over his robes and meditation cushion), forgets things multiple times and struggles to manage his email inbox. With his shortcomings and idiosyncrasies on show, what he has always encouraged me to become seems far more attainable. "It's not about achieving perfection, it's about achieving liberation." This approach also discourages perfectionism by creating an atmosphere of fearlessness and willingness to make mistakes.

Troublesome to the point of abuse

Another potential danger with putting a teacher on a pedestal is that you end up blinding yourself to their faults and start thinking they can do no wrong. Like this, you expose yourself to being taken advantage of. In a close and trusting relationship we must be aware of the potential for that trust to be misdirected, misused or outright abused. Regrettably, it happens. Over the past decade, the #MeToo movement has uncovered a catalogue of abuse from supposed teachers, priests and role models in many areas of life – including, I'm sad to say, in the Buddhist world. These days, teachers who actually practise what they preach and avoid excess and immorality are almost overshadowed in the media by the numerous high-profile cases of "gurus gone wrong". On the flip-side, as a teacher, being put on a pedestal by one of your students can feel like a form of abuse in itself.

As we've said, often the reason people look for a perfect guru figure is to replace something they were missing as a child. They may crave a parent-like figure – someone who's in complete control of the world and can give them safety, security and protection. In response, they might assume a childlike state of unconditional devotion and relinquished responsibility. In effect, they give up charge of their own lives and pass it on to the teacher – a condition sometimes referred to as "guru syndrome". Critics and victims of abusive teachers often point to a culture of secrecy, patriarchy and sexism that has been allowed to build up, and because of the persistent fantasy that they can do no wrong, the community can find it difficult to hold the teacher to account. Furthermore, the sense of collusion or complicity in the acts that took place can create shame on the part of the student, only compounding their reluctance or unwillingness to speak out.

Unfortunately, anxieties around the potential dangers of abuse play into the second area where teachers can become troublesome Buddhas – that of having difficulty with authority or struggling to have faith in the teacher.

Having trouble with authority figures

As already mentioned, attachment theory gives us some ideas about how issues around having trust in a teacher can come about. If an infant experienced any kind of abuse at the hands of their caregivers – be that physical, emotional, sexual or neglectful – then they're much more likely to have problems relating to authority as an adult. For example, if their primary caregiver(s) felt it was better to evoke fear to get them to obey, then the infant may grow up to have uncertain or sceptical feelings toward authority. They may want to trust a teacher but find it difficult to allow themselves to do so. Since that's precisely what happened to the famous 17th-century Japanese Rinzai Zen teacher Bankei Yotaku, I'd like to explore his story here.[21]

Bankei Yotaku

Bankei (1622–93) was born into a low-ranking samurai family. His father was a doctor and he had four brothers and four sisters. The fact that his given name, Muchi, literally means "don't fall behind" gives you a sense of the attitude his parents may have had toward him from the beginning. Muchi was a difficult-to-control, rebellious and mischievous child. His mother discovered one day that if she pretended to die, that would shock little Muchi into behaving. It worked, but we can only imagine what effect it had on him – especially when his father unexpectedly did die. At this point, aged only 11, Muchi attempted suicide by swallowing a large number of spiders which he thought to be poisonous.

The following year he entered school. It seems he enjoyed the philosophy classes (they would have studied the Confucian classics) but hated the calligraphy lessons – so much so that he would skip them and go home instead. His continued misbehaviour began disgracing the family. His mother's shock tactics had stopped working and his older brother, now head of the family, didn't know what to do. In a fit of desperation, he threw Muchi, then aged just 14, out of the house and effectively disowned him.

These historical accounts reveal that the behaviour of Bankei's childhood caregivers was at best confused, and at worst neglectful or emotionally abusive. His responses make it look likely he would have developed an aversion-type behavioural pattern with regard to his close relationships, with elements of avoidance and moments of rebellion or anger.

Thankfully, Muchi was taken in by a kindly neighbour and struggled on for a year or two. When he'd been at school, he'd been struck by a phrase from a Confucian text about "illuminating virtue" and had been pondering it. Someone recommended that he visit the local Zen temple to ask about it. When he arrived, the teacher told him: "You'll only find it within. You need to practise meditation." So Muchi asked to become a monk and was accepted. He stayed at the temple for a couple of years but became disillusioned with the teacher and found nothing that satisfied him. When he was 19, he decided to go travelling in search of another teacher – one who could give him the answer to his question and put his problems to rest.

Given his difficult childhood, it might not come as a surprise that the teenage Muchi would've had problems trusting the authority or guidance of his teacher. He might have craved an intimate and trusting relationship but worried about getting too close for fear of losing it. He might also have deeply doubted himself and his ability to relate to others, and as a result tried to portray himself as independent and self-reliant as a way of compensating.

After an extensive search all across Japan, he arrived back at his home temple aged 23, even more disillusioned and exhausted. With nothing left to lose, he decided to abandon his teacher and build himself a little hermitage, wall himself in using mud plaster and devote every hour to meditation. He practised like this by himself for some years. He later recounted: "I pressed myself without mercy, draining myself mentally and physically." He was certainly extremely determined, but we might imagine this drive came from the deep well of emotional and psychological pain that had built up inside him from his childhood.

As a result of his long hours of meditation, he developed septicaemia in his buttocks and in the end contracted tuberculosis. At age 26, the doctor said he would die soon – so he became resolved to dying. At the point at which he had almost completely given up, he said, "I felt a strange sensation in my throat. I spat against a wall. A mass of black phlegm large as a soapberry rolled down the side" and suddenly his mind-perspective shifted. This was his moment of enlightenment. Fortunately for him the pain and emotional turmoil he suffered ultimately drove him in the direction of Zen – but they might just as easily have led him to a far more destructive ending (and almost did on a number of occasions).

Bankei's childhood taught him that people in authority aren't all on your side and they can do hurtful things to trick you into behaving (for example his mother pretending to die). We can imagine, then, why he might have had quite a troublesome relationship with his first teacher and struggled to take on board his instruction to patiently look within. We can also guess that part of the reason he spent so much effort looking outside himself for the answer to his questions was that he was unconsciously searching for an idealized, nurturing and loving parental figure who could make everything right at the wave of a hand. After his search turned out to be fruitless, he locked himself away in a hut and meditated almost to death. As well as learning not to trust authority figures, his childhood had almost certainly also taught him to become fiercely independent. At this stage, he felt he couldn't rely on anyone but himself.

After his experiences as a youth, Bankei went on to become a brilliant and hugely popular teacher, and remained fiercely devoted to his mother, who actually became a Buddhist nun. He would tell his students how he thought his extreme striving for resolution and enlightenment was misdirected – but the best he knew how to do at the time. As a result, he was always adamant that no one needed to go to the lengths he did, and his teaching became characterized by compassion, gentleness and simplicity.

So what can we learn from Bankei's story? He had a difficult childhood, which likely prompted the behavioural patterns of rebellious independence and intense striving. But it was through this suffering that he was able to find peace. The Buddha taught that there can be no enlightenment without suffering. However bad it might seem, it's only when we are able to fully accept our situation and surrender to our pain, grief, anxiety or anger that we can slowly, lovingly learn to let go of it. Just as light can only exist because of darkness, compassion and wisdom can only exist because of suffering.

Hakuin and Torei

Another historical example of a troublesome spiritual teacher comes from the story of the famous 17th-century Japanese Zen teacher Hakuin Ekaku (1686–1769) and his student Torei Enji (1721–92).[22]

Torei was ordained as a monk when he was 17, and after a series of long, solitary practice sessions in the few years that followed, he gained a number of important insights. He sought out Hakuin when he was 22 years old as someone who could help him further his training.

Hakuin immediately recognized Torei as an exceptional student and a potential Dharma heir (successor). Torei had a burning intention to practise and even wrote a letter to Hakuin in the first few months of arriving at the temple requesting his "iron hammer and tongs" (meaning his most strict and severe teaching). By the time Torei was about 30 years old, Hakuin had developed a hope that he might one day take over running his own temple, Shoin-ji. As a step in that direction, Hakuin asked Torei to take on the abbotship of a tiny, run-down temple called Muryo-ji in a nearby village. However, Torei resisted due to a number of worries. He was concerned about his health. As a result of practising in severe, cold conditions, he had developed tuberculosis and had, not long before, come close to death. He also thought the responsibilities of running a temple would sidetrack him from his own Zen training and he was concerned that his teacher would overly interfere in his running of it. He also didn't want to get trapped, feeling unable to leave, or be coerced into assuming the abbotship at Hakuin's own, much larger temple (and Hakuin did in fact endeavour to coerce him on a number of occasions).

After various compromises and conditions, Torei finally conceded and ended up serving as abbot of Muryo-ji for more than four years. He left after that time because Hakuin was putting increasing pressure on him to take over Shoin-ji and assume the position of his heir. It seems that Hakuin was finally able to empathize when it dawned on him that he felt much the same at Torei's age – with that reluctance to take on responsibility and desire to focus on his own studies. It took a good few years before Torei felt ready again to move toward his teacher. In 1758 they ended up co-leading a series of lectures. This prompted Hakuin to buy the ruined old temple of Ryutaku-ji and ask Torei to restore it and run it as a training temple. Again Torei refused. But Hakuin went ahead with the assumption that Torei would agree eventually. In 1761, an exasperated Torei finally agreed and became the abbot of what became, in the centuries that followed, an important temple in the Rinzai school.

Although we don't know much about Torei's early life and relationship with his parents, he certainly had a rather troubled relationship with his teacher. Along with Torei's obvious resistance to taking on responsibility, Hakuin, like an overbearing parent, had his own ambitions for Torei and tried on multiple occasions to force them on him. During his life, Torei had to learn to balance his desire to practise and deepen his own study with the energy of Hakuin's repeated insistence that he step up and take on responsibility, all with the challenges of managing his own frail health. In the end, Torei became an important Zen master in his own right and a major figure in the revival of the Rinzai school. His teaching career lasted 40 years and during that time he wrote a number of significant books on Zen and completed Hakuin's project to redevelop the koan study curriculum (which remains in use today).

Teachers teach in more ways than one

Reflecting back over this chapter on troublesome teachers, we see that if we're to learn from a teacher, we must first learn to trust them. The seeds of trust might come initially from others having recognized the teacher's level or skill, but as our relationship develops, our willingness to trust them comes to rest more and more on our own experience. However, in any kind of close, adult relationship, it's normal for issues to arise that have their roots in childhood. Some people look for a teacher as a surrogate parent. They may crave things like love, recognition, validation or acceptance, but whether the teacher offers them or not, looking to a teacher as a parent is ultimately a sure-fire path to greater suffering. Some students try to objectify their teacher into a perfect, idealized being, whereas others remain dubious of authority, wanting to trust a teacher but at the same time finding it difficult to allow themselves to do so. A suitably skilled and conscious teacher will not dismiss anything the student feels as wrong or inappropriate; neither will they play to their desires. The teacher's role is to create a safe space in which a student can allow the roots of their suffering (in whatever form that is, however uncomfortable or painful) to arise and be seen, acknowledged and slowly let go of. Ultimately, their job is to help their students develop a deep belief in themselves.

That said, as with any close relationship, it's essential we cultivate trust with our eyes open. If we start holding our teachers up, thinking they're beyond reproach, then we're not fully seeing the truth of what's in front of us, and we also risk exposing ourself to the potential of abuse. It's vital that, no matter how our relationship evolves, we remain able to hold our teachers to account if or where necessary.

Troublesome students

As much as Hakuin was a troublesome teacher for Torei, Torei was probably an equally troublesome student for Hakuin. Many of us find ourselves quite regularly in a teaching role – whether that be at work with a new recruit, or at home with our children – and, if we let them, our troublesome students can also turn into some of our best teachers.

I spoke to Shinkai Roshi, a Zen teacher in Oregon, USA about this subject, and he remembered when he was first setting up his Zen group: "Some of my students really pushed my buttons, but in doing so they very much helped me move into new territory." Over the years, his students have clearly showed him how he needed to let go of trying to control things. "As we got our Zen community going, I had my own ideas about how it should and shouldn't be. But I quickly saw that what I wanted and how things were unfolding were two different things." This divergence revealed some of his preconceived ideas and tendencies toward control. Mirroring the famous sentiment of Dwight Eisenhower (who said "Planning is everything, but the plan is nothing"), Shinkai said: "I thought I always knew what was best and found myself wanting to micromanage everyone, but I recognize now this was just more of my own stuff coming up." What he had imagined wasn't necessarily the direction the community was gravitating toward. "They [his students] showed me that I needed to let go of any notion of it being *my* centre, and let things unfold the way they're meant to unfold. They showed me how important it is to ask for help."

As he's got better at letting go of being in charge, he said he's been able to recognize the deep wisdom of the group. "When you let go, the kindness of others and the universe enters in and amazing things happen." He sees that the community is now evolving in ways he couldn't have imagined, and in ways that are a great benefit to everyone. He concluded: "I can appreciate and am grateful for seeing that there's something so much bigger and all-encompassing that moves through me and everything."

PART THREE

REALLY TROUBLESOME BUDDHAS

CHAPTER 12
OGRE BUDDHAS

There might be some people in your life that fall at the far end of the troublesome spectrum: those that have abused us or caused us profound pain in some way. When the wounds run deep, it's not so easy to accept them as people, let alone acknowledge that they might be able to teach us something about ourselves. Even the idea that they could teach us anything might be repellent. It might just be that you want absolutely nothing to do with them (and sometimes it would certainly be safer). I know how that feels.

The hatred we often feel toward these ogre figures can have tremendous power behind it. Thoughts of what happened and the feelings of simmering anger and revulsion can preoccupy us, perhaps for long periods at a time. Gradually, all life's colours can become tinged by the hue of hate. While the feelings around what they did can seem crystal clear, it might be difficult to see anything beyond them. However, it's been said that hanging on to anger and resentment is like drinking poison and hoping it will kill someone else.[23] It doesn't help, and in the end it will only hurt ourselves.

Trauma or abuse are profound wounds that don't really heal by themselves. Without the right kind of attention, they fester. When we perceive even a hint of something that could aggravate the wound, we recoil, tense up and act in all sorts of ways to pre-emptively protect ourselves. Over time, these actions become habits. The establishment of these habits is like erecting walls to protect us from the perceived dangers of life. We might start distancing ourselves from everyone (just in case we get hurt again), or we might learn to put on a public face – a mask so we can pretend to be someone else; we might start laughing at everything or crying at every opportunity. It doesn't matter how much protection we put up, behind it the wound is still there, unhealed. We may operate like this for years, perhaps even forgetting the details of how the wounds got there – or that they even exist. But they're there nonetheless.

One day, the pain of remaining bound like a crab that has outgrown its shell becomes too great. The risk of remaining like this is more painful than the risk of squeezing out of our old shell. The first step is to acknowledge that uncomfortable, squeezed, constrained feeling – despite the anticipation and fear of what might come next. It's not easy; the easiest thing to do would be to avoid the feeling and distract ourselves. Thus we need to summon great courage. But know that you don't have to do it alone. Lean on your support network, or seek out someone new who can support you through this process (like a psychotherapist or spiritual teacher). Know that if a troublesome person's behaviour ever escalates to the point of abuse, it's crucial that you take appropriate action, not just see it as something to accept passively. But as you soften your discriminations and judgements and gradually let go of any pain, you'll find increased lightness and freedom in your being. When dealing with my own ogres over the years, a line from a poem by the 13th-century Persian poet Rumi has really helped. He said: "The wound is the place where the light enters you." If we can find a way of peeling back the reassuringly familiar, but very possibly calcified, layers of protection, and find the courage to look directly at the wound underneath – without recoiling at the sight of it – we might just be able to peer through the wound, directly into ourselves. This is the true gift that trauma and pain can offer us.

Piercing the skin on my emotional custard

As I mentioned earlier, the person who caused the accident that killed my stepfather and disabled my mother was an off-duty police officer. His name was Michael. From the time of the accident until a good way after I'd started psychotherapy (a period of around ten years), "Michael" was a concept I couldn't get in touch with. Even though I saw him in person in the courtroom a few months after the accident (he was convicted with causing death by dangerous driving and sentenced to a period in prison), it felt like, in my mind, he hung out there somewhere in space, out of reach. During that time, I found it completely impossible to get in touch with any emotions regarding Michael and what he did.

When I first started psychotherapy, I vividly remember some sessions where my therapist asked me how I felt about what he did, and I would say: "Well, it wasn't his fault. It was chance – probability. Yes, he was doing something he oughtn't have been, but he'd probably done it many times before without incident." Essentially, I had rationalized my lack of feeling. My therapist would encourage me, saying it's okay to feel angry. But despite that permission, I continued to justify my response, claiming it wasn't Michael's fault. I remember this eventually prompted a rare emotional retort from my therapist (he was usually good at reflecting on what I said steadily and non-judgementally). He said something like: "Well who else's fault was it? How can you *not* be angry? I just don't get it!" Looking back, it felt like he was attempting to poke a stick through the thick skin I'd grown on all that emotional custard. I'm pretty sure he was trying to provoke me in order to help me get in touch with my feelings.

I spent some months searching, meditating and reflecting on what I felt about Michael. I remember having all sorts of dreams that we explored and talked about. I also remember discussing it for the first time with my mum. Eventually I found traces of anger and disgust, and my therapist encouraged me to begin expressing these feelings inside and outside of the sessions. Seeing that there was actually anger there made me realize that I had a deep fear that if I touched it, my whole being would suddenly explode like an uncontrollable volcano. I was scared my world would fall apart, so I was holding it together by blocking out my feelings. But the reality was that it was actually difficult to touch this anger, and when I did, it felt like wet tinder – it was near impossible to ignite.

Gradually, during the therapy sessions and in my own meditation practice, I opened the lid on my emotional box – anger, resentment and hate timidly crept out. I began to let them find their expression. I found my anger toward Michael, and at the injustice of what happened. "Why me? Why us?" I remember shouting. I raged at the universe and at fate for letting this happen to me and my family. I'd often leave these therapy sessions a quivering wreck – but, importantly, my world didn't fall apart.

I can't remember the exact point that I felt able to forgive Michael for what he did – it crept up on me slowly. Looking back now, I'm certain there would have been no way of arriving at the point of forgiveness if I hadn't gone through that period of getting in touch with my anger and the blame and learning to express it. True forgiveness is not a method of bypassing that stage – it's an act of genuine acceptance and letting go. Nor is feeling and expressing anger bad or nasty or wrong. For me, getting in touch with my anger and realizing its full intensity was a necessary step along the path. We can't let go of something that we're not able to fully acknowledge.

The experience of bringing the concept of "Michael" down from hanging in space and into arm's reach, getting in touch with the raw feelings I had for him and what he did, letting them go and finally forgiving him, wasn't too rocky a process in the end – at least compared with the experience of forgiving my abusive father. But it was through finding and allowing myself to feel anger toward Michael that I realized a big proportion of my anger was actually directed toward my father.

Forgiving my father

Before the age of six, for probably some years, my father played sexual games with me. When mum found out, she went straight to the police and he was immediately expelled from the house. In the years that followed, we only saw him under supervision. Shortly after it all became public, my sister and I saw a child psychologist who interviewed us and wrote a report on what they thought happened and what effect it might've had on us. Mum kept copies of the reports, which she showed me when I started psychotherapy.

In my 20s, a complicated chaos of mixed-up feelings had formed around my father (much of which I'd repressed). I came to understand that these had been shaped by different influences. One was the accident and its aftermath. Essentially the accident had eclipsed all that had gone on before in my life – it had ended the close relationship I'd developed with my stepfather and put a kibosh on my process of coming to terms with my childhood abuse. The other big one was, of course, my mother. As we grew up, her opinions of my father, her emotions (including her guilt over what had happened), as well as her own individual hang-ups and worldviews, all rubbed off on us. She always described herself as naïve; she told me one of the reasons she married was in order to enable her to leave the parental home, and that she had children partly in an attempt to bolster her relationship with my father.

Ever since he left, my father has remained a recurring presence in my life – mostly around birthdays and particularly relating to the issue of money. For example, when I was younger he'd often help fund expensive birthday gifts and contribute various lump sums now and then to help pay for things like university. As a result (and this was probably also influenced by mum), I developed a sense of what I deserve from him – I felt "I deserve an apology for his actions", and "I deserve money in compensation for his abuse and subsequent absence". I also developed an odd sense of duty toward him – as in "I should tell him what I'm up to because he's my father".

When I was about 25, prompted by the psychotherapy process, I began writing to my father asking about what he remembered about the abuse. He insisted the sexual games I remembered happened only once, and that was by accident. He said it had been initiated by me and that I had enjoyed the game. At this point I had already begun to touch into my reservoir of repressed anger, and his claims incited outrage in me. What he said went against what little I could actually remember and what was described in the psychologist's reports.

As a five-year-old, of course I wanted attention and enjoyed playing games with my parents. But to be told that something that I liked doing was wrong was totally confusing to my young self. I wanted my dad, but people were saying he was bad and he had to be taken away. My mum remembers that I cried and cried for him every time we said goodbye. In the months following his initial expulsion, I had a number of sessions with the child psychologist to help me process this, but I suspect this wasn't enough. A few years later, I innocently tried playing the same sexual games with my stepfather and, as mum later told me, he was good at helping me understand why that wasn't appropriate.

Through psychotherapy and my meditation practice, I had to learn to comfort those aspects of myself that had been repressed or had retreated into the dark recesses of my consciousness and hadn't been allowed to grow up. It was about creating a non-judgemental presence in which I could put a metaphorical arm around myself and allow whatever was to arise to surface and be seen. At first this was facilitated by my therapist and through guided meditation practice, but gradually I learnt to internalize

it and practise it alone. During this time I remember being
on a meditation retreat, and one morning, right in the middle
of one of my meditation sessions, I had a vision of a monster
jumping out from under a bed, right into my face. It came out
of nowhere and felt extremely scary; I was viscerally shaken
and I couldn't close my eyes again for the rest of the practice.
Afterwards, my teacher helped me to see the vision through
my adult eyes. I realized it was only scary to my inner child's
perspective. This was a powerful lesson in how to reframe all
that I remembered from my childhood – all that I saw as a
child through my childish-perception – so I could see it, and
begin relating to it, through my grown-up eyes.

Since what my father admitted conflicted with what little
I could actually remember and I had been told, I went through
a long period of being angry with him. I wanted to know:
"Why can't he just admit it? Why does he always have to
bend the truth?" After some years I came to the conclusion
that, over time, he has probably come to accept his version
of events as his truth. It's quite possible that when he told me
it only happened once, he may not have been consciously
lying. Regardless, after a long time of hunting relentlessly for
"the truth", I realized there really is no one truth – I have my
truth and he has his truth. And I've come to accept that.

As he's grown older I've started to see him in a different
way. His hair has gone white, his shoulders are hunched and
his face is more wrinkled; I've grown and he looks somehow
smaller now. What happened, happened, and, at this point in
my journey of healing, I don't need to know any more details
than I know already. Whether he can say sorry and fully repent
for all that he did no longer worries me. He's a product of
his past and the psychological protection mechanisms that
came into play for him, of his parents and their parents and
of society as a whole. As was my mum, and as am I. All this
helped me, over time, to edge toward a sense of forgiveness.
The last time I met with him, I felt ready to say "I forgive
you". I'm not sure what he made of it, or whether he fully

understood, but it felt like a major turning point for me. And I feel confident of the veracity of that feeling, since from then on, it has only grown.

Over the years, I've tried to move toward him enough times that I know I'll just get the same infuriating, not quite honest and often subtly manipulative attitude in return. Some time ago I went through a period of no contact, but I don't feel the need to be so militant any more. I just don't feel drawn to seeing him and I no longer feel a duty or obligation to do so. Just because I've forgiven him doesn't mean I now want to get to know him. But who knows if that might change as life goes on.

As I've opened up to others about my experiences, I've encountered many other people with similar stories of ogre-type troublesome Buddhas and their difficulties with coming to terms with them. Here's a short example from a friend about her journey of approaching her mother about what had happened to her as a child. It illustrates the importance of putting down the weapon of blame for long enough that both parties can feel safe enough to talk openly and honestly.

Washing away the shit

Jess had always had a difficult relationship with her mother. A period of insomnia and bad dreams prompted her to start seeing a psychotherapist and begin examining some of the unresolved issues in their relationship. She said: "It felt like a big rock that you had to pick up and look underneath." The biggest question for her was: "Why didn't you [her mum] protect me when I was being abused as a child?"

She always knew that if you don't work on your issues, then nothing will change in your relationships. "This is easier said than done. You can't just choose to rid yourself of all that history and emotion overnight, you don't know how long it's going to take." In the end, the process she went through in psychotherapy took over three years. "First, I had to deal with my blame. Once I stopped blaming, I realized we could both feel safe enough to lower our defences and begin talking properly." During this period, she brought up the same stuff with her mum repeatedly. She said: "It took a real perseverance on my part." She felt her mum needed to have the same conversations multiple times to help her approach things slowly. "My mother's willingness to talk again and again about what happened and how I felt – to finally look at it full on – made her a Buddha in my eyes."

Jess related how her mother finally admitted that she had been selfish, and didn't see what was truly happening. In the end she said she was sorry. It has deeply surprised Jess that this level of resolution had been possible after 20 years.

Recently she was with her father, looking at photos of when she was little, and happily remembering some of the beautiful moments. She said it was like "Washing away the shit". She went on: "I trust that as I continue to let go of the grudges and anger, all that shit will eventually wash away completely."

Dealing with ogres

Coming to terms with those people at the far end of the troublesome spectrum takes a good deal of time, patience and gentleness toward yourself. Sometimes it requires us to move away, to create distance and strong boundaries – for example, I stopped all communication with my father for a number of years so I could examine my feelings without them getting any more muddied. However, sometimes it might feel appropriate to move toward those people and open the lines of communication.

Along the way, a crucial step is to acknowledge the full extent of your emotions and allow their power to flow through you – however and whatever they may be. Too often, I think, people believe that negative emotions like anger, hate and resentment are bad, and having them is a sign we're not healing. If we're trying to heal the wound, they might think, why would we wrench it open and make it hurt more? But before we can ever hope to begin healing, it's necessary to peel off the old, hardened bandages, and, as Rumi suggests, allow the light to enter you – to look into the wound that's lain underneath, hidden from view for all these years. For me at least, getting in touch with my anger and realizing its full intensity was a necessary step on this path. Sometimes things have to get worse – more painful – before they can get better. Of course, in reality things don't actually get more painful, it's just that we start to become more consciously aware of the pain that's already there – and that increasing awareness is the crux of the mindfulness approach.

Another important step is to take responsibility for our own feelings and stop blaming others. Carl Jung referred to this as "withdrawing the projection of our own shadow onto others". As we've heard, it's only when you stop blaming that both parties can feel safe enough to speak openly and things can begin to move forward. This includes not blaming yourself.

It's important to appreciate that different parts of our mind, personality and consciousness grow up at different rates. Traumatic events can arrest the development of some parts of our being altogether. In the practice of Zen and mindfulness, we don't try to educate or change these parts of our self. Our job is to provide time and space for those stuck or suffering inner-child aspects to be acknowledged, seen and fully accepted. Only once they're fully accepted will they naturally grow up to join the rest of your adult mind. This is a process of learning how to reframe your childhood memories – all that you saw as a child through your child-perception – so you can see them, and begin relating to them, through your grown-up eyes.

For me, it's been a long process of discovery, denial, pain, exploration, confusion, conversation, acceptance and letting go. I've come to realize that for me, right now, it's no longer about what my father did or didn't do, or whose truth is more right. It's about acknowledging how I feel without wanting it to be any different. When we can allow things to be just as they are, then we're in a place to forgive. But remember, forgiving someone doesn't lessen the gravity of what they did or indicate you want to become friends with them – or even speak to them again. Forgiveness means realizing that remaining angry, hateful or blameful doesn't actually punish the other person for what they did, it only hurts you. Forgiveness means opening our hands and putting down the heavy burden of that resentment. As a result, life will feel lighter and freer.

CHAPTER 13
SELF BUDDHAS

By now I'm sure you've got a sense that our work regarding troublesome people is really all about the self and how we relate to it. In essence, the only troublesome Buddha you really ever have is yourself. However, there are a number of specific areas around the troublesome self that I'd like to draw out and explore here.

First, off, the hardest person to bring kindness and compassion to is yourself. Forgiving an ogre can often feel easier than forgiving yourself. Being kind and compassionate toward yourself means loving yourself, and, as with anyone, falling in love takes time, trust and honesty. If, in the past, you've never given yourself those things (or never been given them by others) then self-compassion won't come easily – at least at first. It's important to cut yourself plenty of slack and take things gently. Remember, it's your intention that's the most important thing.

Accepting your own traits

One way we can easily become our own troublesome Buddha is if we're not able to accept our many innate character traits, idiosyncrasies and limitations.

Here's an example from my own life. I've recently started making my own pizza dough. Not long ago, my wife and I were in the kitchen and I was attempting to stretch out the dough into a baking tray while she was preparing the toppings. As we were chatting, my fingers kept on getting caught on the sticky dough. I added more flour, and pressed out some more. Suddenly I tore a hole in an area I'd made too thin. As I tried to patch it up, trying not to get my fingers stuck again, we kept on talking. I saw that as much as I stretched out one side of the dough, the other side contracted back. I was getting more and more frustrated at the fiddly actions not going right. My face was flushing and my body was getting hot as the frustration energy rose. Just as I was about to criticize my wife for something ridiculous like chopping too loudly, I managed to hold my tongue. With some effort, I was able to maintain enough emotional regulation – accepting what I felt but consciously influencing the expression of those feelings – to avoid unjustifiably exploding at my wife. Of course she wasn't chopping too loudly – I had just reached boiling point!

Ever since I was a child, I've always found finicky manual tasks frustrating (I could never have become a surgeon!). However, I've not always been sufficiently aware to be able to curb my rising frustration and avoid lashing out. As a teenager, my mum eventually stopped asking me to do any DIY tasks because experience had taught her that I would become extremely irritable and unpleasant as a result of my frustration. Over the years I've had to accept that certain manual tasks will frustrate the hell out of me.

These days, in general, I do get less irritable because I've learnt to notice and allow the initial seedlings of emotional frustration to arise and be acknowledged, rather than be suppressed or ignored (thus allowing them to grow out of control beneath my consciousness). I've also learnt to accept that fiddly work will frustrate me – that's just part of who I am. The pizza-dough event I described has turned all the subsequent pizza-dough-making sessions into fantastic opportunities to cultivate my skills in mindfulness and acceptance!

Here's another example from a friend, Oliver, who is a Zen practitioner and, by nature, thoroughly absent minded.

Stealing other people's time

By his own admission, Oliver would often leave lights on at the language school where he worked, leave doors unlocked and lose books, wallets and keys on a regular basis. He said: "My manager would be quick to remind me how my forgetfulness makes things difficult for others." He went on: "By contrast, one of the other teachers who was efficient and good at remembering everything would often express their annoyance with me and claim that I was 'stealing their time'." Oliver used to think: "When they get angry at me for being forgetful, what can I do? I'm not doing it on purpose. How am I going to accept myself for who I am when I feel guilty for just being myself?"

Oliver continued: "In the beginning, you just promise yourself that you won't do it again – then you do. And again!" With time he's realized the importance of taking responsibility for his actions, even though they weren't intentional. "I've started to admit to myself and the others when I've messed up. Developing my relationship with myself has been an ongoing process – at the same time accepting who I am right now and trying to do what I can to improve myself for the future."

These days he's grateful for the more efficient people in his life. "They show me the blind spots in my attention." He reflected: "I've had to really open myself to the people that I've annoyed and say sorry." But this has taken some time, and, he said, "I've had to do it on several occasions". Through this process, he said he now understands himself much better and, over the years, has found a great deal of improvement in his absent-mindedness. "Last year I mislaid a textbook only once or twice!"

It's not easy when we have our character flaws pointed out to us as clearly as happened to Oliver. It's so tempting to take up a defensive position, trying to justify our actions – both to others and to ourselves. But it's only through learning to accept our foibles – what we get wrong and what we're not so good at (and honestly apologizing when we inconvenience or hurt someone else) – that we find the teacher within our own selves and edge closer to who we genuinely are. We learn to take off the protective masks and express a deeper honesty, both inwardly and outwardly.

Opinions

Another big area of difficulty regarding the troublesome Buddha of our self revolves around our opinions. In a sense, opinions can be seen as distinct from thoughts or emotions; they're views, judgements or assessments formed in the mind about a particular matter, but may well arise because of a series of thoughts and/or emotions.

First, I want to emphasize that it's important and totally natural to form opinions – just as long as we remain aware that that's what they are: just opinions. The Buddha was keenly aware of this. He admitted that while some views are limiting, others can be helpful, especially in moving us forward on the spiritual path.[24] Opinions only start to become troublesome when we begin holding onto them. The Buddha said: "Those who cling to perceptions and views wander the world offending people."[25] When we lose sight of the fact that our opinions are just opinions, they creep toward becoming beliefs and we cease being open to other angles and perspectives. We end up defending our staunch position because that's what we've hooked our wagon to. The technical way to describe this is to say we've "identified" with them. I'm sure we've all been on the receiving end of this when a conversation turns from a debate into a polemic. At this point the other person has stopped being interested in your views and just wants to persuade you that their opinions are right and win the argument. Ultimately, holding onto opinions only acts to confine us.

Although the Buddha appreciated that some views can be helpful, he thought that ultimately all views and opinions should be discarded. In describing this, he used an analogy – he said helpful views are like a raft that enables us to cross a river to get to the further shore (which in his view is the shore of awakening). Once the raft's job is done, though, it should be abandoned, not carried around and shown off.[26]

Opinions and beliefs are tricky to work with. It's sometimes difficult to recognize that we hold certain beliefs because they're so deeply ingrained into our worldview. I think a great way of testing how lightly you hold your opinions is through debates with other people. If your discussions regularly turn into tirades and you frequently feel compelled to convince the other party that you're right and they're wrong, then this is a good indicator that your opinions may have solidified a little too much. How would it be to approach the discussion with the intention first to understand and then to be understood? And then look for ways to bridge the differences between your opinions – as opposed to seeking to entrench your views.

Some parts of society tend to judge someone who doesn't bring along with them a cart-load of opinions about all manner of things as being flimsy, boring, vacuous or perhaps even morally weak. But being aware of our opinions and holding them lightly gives us the freedom to be in a place of ambiguity and paradox where conflicting truths may lie side-by-side.

Many teachers have written about the importance of letting go of our opinions. The third Chinese ancestor of Zen, Sengcan, wrote in his poem *Xinxin Ming* (Verses on the Faith-Mind): "Do not search for the truth; only cease to cherish opinions."[27] We also know the great Zen master Joshu often liked to quote

the opening few lines of this same poem, since it really gets to
the heart of the matter:

> The Great Way is not difficult for those who have
> no preferences.
>   When love and hate are both absent everything
> becomes clear and undisguised.
>   Make the smallest distinction, however, and
> you are as far from it as heaven is from earth.[28]

Delusions

From a young age we develop ideas about ourselves which,
whether right or wrong, plausible or implausible, kind or
unkind, in short order become fixed into our minds. For
example, when Katy was seven, a cousin rudely remarked that
she had a big nose. By the age of 13 she hated seeing her face
in profile, and by the age of 22 she'd saved enough money to
pay for a nose job. It doesn't matter how big her nose actually
was, the belief grew strong enough that she willingly paid for
an operation to change it.

In Buddhism, ideas that become fixed into beliefs are called
delusions. The world is not fixed; things are in a constant state
of flux. Anything that we attempt to solidify or objectify in
any way must necessarily be false. One of the fundamental
delusions that Buddhism points to is that of seeing our self as
fixed and unchanging. We may even have a sense that we're
actually unchangeable.

The unconscious self likes to believe that we'll forever stay
young and healthy, even when it knows that's an impossibility
– one thing we can be certain of is that we'll fall ill now and
then, grow old and eventually die. Even when we notice those
first few grey hairs it can be hard for our whole being to accept
that we aren't a permanent, unchanging entity (even at the
point of lying on our death bed).

To objectify, concretize, fixate or hold on to something will always, in the end, lead to pain. For example, you've had your favourite pair of jeans for years and they've always fitted amazingly and are exceptionally comfortable. So when they start to wear out, you find it difficult to accept. You go on wearing them thinking that the worn-out patches actually make the jeans look better, whereas in fact they've now gone way beyond cool and have started to sag unflatteringly. Holding on always causes more pain than letting go. Holding on means we're deluding ourselves; it means we're not really seeing the world as it is, but as a fantasy version.

When beliefs become fixed, things turn out differently to what we expected or wanted and we become dissatisfied, disappointed and frustrated. This is how our troublesome self causes us suffering. The antidote to this is awareness. Awareness brings to light the ideas, concepts and thoughts that have become frozen in our mind, and we start to see the unhelpful habits, reactions and behaviours that we've adopted in response to them.

And as we notice more, it's absolutely essential that we bring to that awareness an attitude of non-judgement and openness. When we're able to bring an open, accepting awareness to the present moment, then we start to see things closer to what they really are.

I'd like to close this chapter with a short practice of self-compassion.

Practice of self-compassion

Sit in a comfortable, upright posture. Make sure you feel aligned, balanced and relaxed. Let your gaze softly rest on these words. Let go of any tension in your face and shoulders and relax into your belly.

Scan your body for any physical feelings of discomfort or pain. Maybe there's something immediately obvious, or maybe not. Take your time. If you notice multiple areas of discomfort, try to find the most intense area. See if you can put your attention right in the middle of this sensation. If that's too much, then perhaps choose an area next to the zone of intensity.

Discomfort and pain are not pleasant sensations, but instead of instinctively recoiling as we might do usually, try to be curious about them: is the sensation sharp or broad? Is it constant or dancing about (perhaps throbbing)? Is it heavy or light? Does it have a colour associated with it? Try to stay with this discomfort like you might do with a close friend, viewing it with as much kindness and patience as you can. Metaphorically put your arm around the pain and sit next to it. It's not wrong to have pain in your body; pain is a messenger. What message might your pain be communicating? There's no need to try to work anything out – just listen.

Now let go of your attention on the discomfort. Put your hands over your heart (or any other area of the body that feels soothing to you). Feel the gentle touch and notice what effect that gesture has on your body. Acknowledge that you're not always as kind to yourself and others as you could be. How would it be to forgive yourself for all your mistakes and fallibilities? Say to yourself: "I forgive myself." Make a resolution right now to do your best not to make these same mistakes again.

Say to yourself: "May I accept myself as I am. May I be kind and loving. May I be healthy, happy and at peace."

Part 4 is all about how we see through the illusion of a separate, unchanging self and wake up to the dynamic reality of interconnection, emptiness and oneness. By doing this, we can begin to see the troublesome people in our lives as Buddhas – as troublesome Buddhas.

PART FOUR

SEEING TROUBLESOME
PEOPLE AS BUDDHAS

CHAPTER 14
REALIZING BUDDHA-NATURE

In Part 1, I discussed the metaphor of a mountain range enveloped in cloud, with the rocky peaks protruding through the top of the cloudy veil. The view of seeing many separate distinct mountain peaks represents our conventional perspective. From this viewpoint we see different people, distinguish houses from trees, lakes and tables, and differentiate the flavours of chocolate and coffee. This is the world of duality, division and discrimination, and it is where many of us live for most if not all of the time. Discrimination is important: it allows us to judge what's healthy and what's poisonous, and determine what's appropriate. It also allows us to perceive pleasure, pain and suffering. But it comes with a price. Discrimination describes a world of separation. We think "I am different from you", which instinctively leads to an attitude of self-centred protectionism – we think "I need to safeguard myself because the big universe is a hostile place". We perceive the world in terms of what are known as "zero-sum games" – meaning when you win or gain something like money or fame, someone else loses (and thus the total sum remains zero). Believing that the world is made of separate things is a path that will ultimately lead to suffering and unhappiness.

However, there is another perspective. As we mentioned in the mountain-range metaphor, when the clouds clear away, we can see how the mountaintops are actually connected to one other via the valley floors. The mountains are all part of the one range – equivalently, you and I, houses, tables and chocolates, are all connected and just different parts, or manifestations, of the whole. To get a sense of this different view, try to determine where the edge of your body is. "Surely it's my skin" you say – but what about the heat that radiates off your skin? Is that "yours"? And what about your breath? At what point does it become "you" and "not you"? These are just the physical aspects; what about ideas and memories? When you taught your colleague how to reset the printer when it malfunctioned, is that idea "yours"? When does it stop becoming yours? It's impossible to say. These questions orient us toward the world of oneness, non-duality and emptiness. Your skin, your breath and your ideas aren't separate things – they're all expressions of this one universe. From this perspective, the universe is not full of distinct objects, but of dynamic processes, interlinked, interdependent and arising together. This is what "emptiness" really means in a Buddhist context.

This non-dual, impermanent, interdependent view is what the Buddha awoke to all those centuries ago (the word Buddha means "awakened one"). He saw that the only reason anything exists is because everything in the universe is interconnected and in a constant state of change. It's for this reason that Buddhists refer to this fundamental, universal, shared characteristic of change as Buddha-nature. It's something we all have. But, unfortunately, not many people realize it. Buddha-nature, therefore, has a dual meaning – it means that quality of non-separateness, but it also refers to the underlying potential in all of us to see or wake up to this perspective – just as the Buddha did.

Strictly, Buddha-nature isn't actually something we have, but something we are. It surpasses all concepts of this and that, knowing and not knowing, or right and wrong. It just is (and has always been and will always be). Yes, it may be temporarily obscured by our conditioned behaviours, beliefs, attachments and constrictions, but it's always there – just like the sun when it goes behind a bank of cloud.

What does it mean to see someone else's Buddha-nature?

Just like you, the people we find troublesome in our lives are each manifestations of this one universe. Each of us is like a facet in a giant jewel – different facets, but one jewel. Perceiving people like this means seeing *their* true nature or Buddha-nature. In Zen, there are a number of koans designed to help us to step into this way of seeing things. One is "Mr Chang drinks wine, Mr Li gets drunk".[29] From a conventional viewpoint, this statement makes no sense. How can Mr Li get drunk when it's Mr Chang that drinks wine? If this happened regularly, Mr Li might find Mr Chang troublesome! But from a non-dualistic, non-discriminative viewpoint, Mr Li and Mr Chang are as separate as your left hand is from the right, or as one mountain peak is from another. When Mr Chang drinks, not just Mr Li gets drunk but the entire universe does. This is because Mr Chang and Mr Li are not distinct, isolated objects, but two sides of the one coin. Equivalently, when you say or do something nasty, the person on the receiving end suffers – but actually so do you and so does the entire cosmos. Because we're so deeply interconnected and interdependent, any action, however small, affects everything else. It's like the allegory of the butterfly that flaps its wings in South America and causes a storm in Europe.

As we've said previously, when we encounter any kind of challenging behaviour, we instinctively assume we're under threat. Our stance toughens up and our reactions become defensive. Because survival depends on our ability to accurately discriminate, any kind of threat will automatically send us into the dualistic, separative worldview. That's why it's so hard, in the heat of the moment, to maintain a sense of the non-dualistic perspective. And that's why we practise. First, we practise finding (and then maintaining) the perspective of oneness in easy, non-threatening situations – like meditating in the comfort of your own home. Then, little-by-little, we learn to keep touch with that perspective in more and more challenging situations, as our threat sense gets activated and we feel that instinctive wish to close in or tighten up.

Buddha-nature is always there. It's not something we get or lose. It's part of what we are. It just gets obscured or hidden under layers of crud (suffering). Those people with more layers of crud are suffering more. Their troublesome behaviour is really an indicator of their underlying pain. So instead of shunning those people or getting angry with them for being irritating or hateful, we actually need to be more compassionate toward them. We need to act with more kindness, sensitivity, patience and tolerance to them, not less. I know this isn't easy – especially when they don't see (or can't accept) your kindness and criticize or throw it back at you. It takes a great deal of courage and strength to stay aware of a troublesome person's Buddha-nature and remain kind and compassionate in your responses to them.

Fortunately, the crud that obscures and disguises our true nature has the potential to become extremely fertile compost. Traditionally, the lotus flower has come to symbolize Buddha-nature. Lotus flowers like growing in muddy ponds, and, in this image, the mud represents our suffering. Under the right conditions, the dormant lotus seed, buried in the mud, can sprout. It still might be a long time before the seedling finds its way out of the murky mire and heads toward the light. However, when it does break the water's surface (representing the moment when we realize our true nature), a beautiful flower will blossom. Without the muck there would be no flower, yet the flower, once above the surface and unfurled in the sun, is left unsullied by the mud. When interacting with a troublesome person, how would it be to focus not on the crud (the things that annoy or irritate you, the spiteful remarks or selfish behaviours), but on the potential in them for that lotus flower to grow and blossom? In my experience, this opens up a totally new way of seeing all other people, including those we find most difficult.

Even those who have abused you or caused you deep pain have Buddha-nature. It may feel very much like they're separate from you – maybe you even want them to be as separate from you as possible – but the truth is they're not. Wanting them to be separate only creates more suffering for you. I know it can be extremely difficult to even entertain the possibility of this perspective when they've perpetrated such terrible things. But it doesn't matter how much physical or emotional distance you try to put between you and them, fundamentally they are still as much part of this one universe as you are. You cannot cut them out of reality. Knowing this doesn't make their actions right, or excuse or lessen the pain they've caused you in any way. But when we come to see the inseparability of the universe, we have to appreciate that includes everything – from the most beautiful and pleasurable to the most ugly and painful. How might it be if you were to relate to these abusive ogres on the level of their Buddha-nature? It may have been buried decades ago by mountains of pain, desires, attachments and beliefs, but underneath all that, it's there.

Acting from this realization

If we recognize that the actions of the people we find troublesome are fundamentally coming from a place of suffering – from the layers of crud that cover and obscure their true nature – what would be the wisest and most intelligent way of responding to that suffering? What would be the kindest way to respond to them?

There's a Zen koan that encourages us to look directly at this conundrum: "What is the samadhi of Kannon?" We encountered Kannon in chapter 4. Kannon is the Japanese name for Avalokiteshvara, the *bodhisattva* (meaning "enlightened being" or embodiment) of compassion, who bears witness to the suffering of the world and takes any and all kind-hearted actions to alleviate it. *Samadhi* is a Sanskrit word that literally means "to collect" or "bring together". In Buddhism it's often used to mean one-pointed meditative absorption or single-minded concentration.

However, in the Zen school samadhi is used in two ways: there's the absorbed, one-pointed concentration found through still meditation, and then there's samadhi in action. This koan uses samadhi in the latter sense – doing what needs to be done from the mind of enlightenment and compassion. Actions taken from the mind of samadhi are different from the actions we take normally. Most of the time, we act for selfish reasons – whether we're conscious of that or not – like wanting recognition or thanks, or trying to get something in return. Actions made from the mind of samadhi are not done with any thought of what should or shouldn't happen, what other people might think or because we're looking for a reward. Zen master Hakuin was a big proponent of this kind of samadhi. He used to say: "Meditation in the midst of activity is a thousand times superior to meditation in stillness."[30]

That's not to say that everyone is always going to be happy with actions taken through samadhi – but the action itself is not the chief factor; the important thing is your state of mind at the time of the acting. Enlightened actions are made with the underlying intention of relieving suffering, and never with the intention of creating more suffering. Just like a boat creates a pattern of disturbed and choppy water as it moves, selfish actions create a turbulent aftermath of suffering (whether that's felt immediately or sometime down the line). That's why in Buddhism it's said that "enlightened action leaves no wake". When we speak or act with the intention of reducing suffering, then the heart will be left at peace. But leaving no wake doesn't mean actions made from samadhi have no consequences. The right word or gesture made lovingly at the right time has the potential to bring great solace or deep insight that can change the course of a life.

The traditional example that illustrates the samadhi of Kannon is the action of reaching behind your head in the middle of the night and adjusting your pillow[31] – just as you might do for a sick person asleep in a hospital bed, or for your partner whose pillow is about to fall off the bed. Since they're asleep they're not going to thank you, or even know you've done anything. You do it naturally, spontaneously, and out of love and a wish to relieve suffering.

The thing about samadhi in action is that we can never force it – if we force it, it is no longer samadhi in action. Enlightened action begins to happen spontaneously only after we've got a good grounding in samadhi in stillness (the one-pointed concentration mentioned above). We must first develop a stable awareness of our present-moment experience through meditation (in a non-threatening environment with minimal distractions). Through this awareness, we examine who we are: our habits and wants, including why we might crave recognition or thanks for actions we take, and our sense of identity. Once we establish a steadfast willingness to recognize and accept the suffering we encounter in this world, including in ourselves, then we can cultivate a deep, unselfish wish to alleviate that suffering and begin doing whatever is needed.

In chapter 4, we came across the Zen parable of two monks who encountered a young woman who needed help crossing a river. The senior monk picked up the woman and carried her on his shoulders across the torrent, but for some time afterwards the junior monk fumed about what had happened because his companion had broken the monastic rules about touching women. In effect, the woman had become his troublesome Buddha.

This is an excellent example of when compassionate action can trump the rules and regulations. Guided by his insight and grounding in awareness and compassion, the senior monk decided he could temporarily disregard the rules in order to help this woman. However, had the junior monk done this without such a grounding in self-awareness and wisdom, it may have done more harm than good (the reason the rules about touching women exist is to keep monks' thoughts on the straight and narrow). The moral of this story is that, before we start looking deeply and honestly into ourselves, spontaneous actions can often be driven by unexamined wants and desires – even if they appear to be compassionate. But once we've developed sufficient wisdom, acceptance and clear seeing, spontaneous action becomes the samadhi of Kannon.

CHAPTER 15
FINDING YOUR SANCTUARY

Elisabeth Kübler-Ross said: "Beautiful people do not just happen."[32] To be mindful is to be aware of what's going on in the present moment around and inside us, while putting aside value judgements like "this is better" or "this is worse". We all have fleeting moments of mindfulness at various points in our day, but to remain mindful over a more sustained period takes effort and practice. Moreover, it's hard enough staying open and consciously aware of our feelings when we're in a comfortable and non-threatening environment, so what about maintaining this in the face of someone whose behaviour you find difficult? As the emotional energy of a situation rises, our instincts and habits start taking over and, as we've discussed, it becomes harder and harder to stay fully aware and not become distressed or overwhelmed by our emotions. It gets difficult to stay emotionally regulated and act from this place. That's why I'd say being mindful around troublesome people is advanced practice!

The fact that you've read this book is a testament to your wish to change the way you approach troublesome people and learn from these difficult encounters. To know that that wish is alive in you deeply moves me. Thank you for wanting to be a kinder and wiser human being. Even if we fly off the handle now and then and say something regretful, if we have that intention firmly established, then we know we're moving in the right direction.

We've looked at how, at the beginning of a troublesome encounter, we can quickly fall into adopting an attitude of "you're wrong and I'm right". But we've also seen that bringing just a little awareness and honesty to the situation shows us that there's more going on than that simple dichotomy. Mindfulness shows us how we bring our own history, beliefs and habits to the situation as much as the other person does. That doesn't excuse their behaviour, but we've seen how the emotions that troublesome people incite in us – the irritation, anger or pain – can be indicators or markers that suggest that there may be something more to learn. Troublesome encounters can be like mirrors: if we're willing to look honestly enough, they show us where we're caught in habitual reactions, skewed perceptions or acting from fixed beliefs or opinions. Like this, difficult people become our Buddhas-of-the-moment.

We've discussed how and why, in the heat of the moment, it can be difficult to stay calm and avoid flipping your lid or lashing out. First, as the brain detects threat, the body switches into "survival mode". This happens with any *perceived* threat, whether that be real or anticipated, physical, social or mental (imagined). The body prepares for the threat by instinctively initiating a fight or flight reaction (boosting the heart rate, tightening the muscles and narrowing the attention), thus wrenching control away from our conscious brain. Second, the jumble of chaotic, conflicting emotions that a troublesome encounter might generate can become so tangled that it becomes difficult to work out what's up and what's down. However, we can learn to better regulate ourselves, both individually and with the help of others, through applying our skills of attention and awareness and responding wisely. It's important to remember, though, that as emotions run high, regulating ourselves takes increasing mental resources. That's why we should cut ourselves a little slack, especially when we're otherwise busy or have additional demands in our life.

When it comes down to it, dealing with troublesome people more wisely is really about dealing with ourselves more wisely. When we start to pay attention, we see that almost everyone behaves in a certain default pattern when it comes to difficult people. Some are wanting or needy, others typically get angry or try to avoid conflict at all costs. Others still operate from misperceptions or misunderstandings that they think are real. Often what makes people difficult is that they spark off or resonate with things within ourselves that we haven't fully accepted or let go of yet. Our job, therefore, is to allow our troublesome encounters to show us how we react out of fear or misunderstanding, where we're holding on to presumptions or fixed opinions and where we're avoiding the truth. Once we see these things, we can learn to accept ourselves more fully with compassion and light-heartedness. Knowing and accepting ourselves will necessarily have a huge effect on how we empathize and respond to difficult people.

In Zen, seeing and accepting your own suffering, letting go of your regrets and making a resolve to be more compassionate and wise in the future is called *sange* (*san* is the Japanese for regret, *ge* means resolve). In the process of *sange* we don't reject our past thoughts, feelings and actions. We appreciate how everything we have ever done – kind or hateful, ignorant or wise – has led us to this moment. And this is the moment where you decide to let go of your regrets – all your grudges and grievances, shame and disappointments – and make a commitment to be wiser and more loving in the future. Being willing to face what we've done and to take responsibility for it is an important step in our practice.

The next koan we're going to explore points very much in this direction. The story goes that a monk once said to Joshu:

"I have just entered this monastery. I beg you to teach me."
Joshu asked: "Have you eaten your rice porridge?" "I have",
replied the monk. "Then," said Joshu, "go and wash your
bowl." At this, the monk had an awakening.

The monk asking the question probably wasn't a total
beginner. There's a strong tradition in Zen for monks to
travel widely and seek out important teachers (like Joshu)
to ask for their teaching. Each master, or course, presents the
teaching in their own way and it was well understood that
a fresh perspective can sometimes precipitate a major shift in
awareness. So this monk probably had a few years under his belt,
but at the beginning of the meeting he obviously still hadn't
quite understood the essence of Zen. One might guess that the
exchange happened just after breakfast (rice porridge – *okayu*
– is a common breakfast dish in Zen temples consisting of hot,
watery rice, sometimes with added beans, often eaten with
ground sesame seasoning and slices of pickled radish). When
the monk asks for Joshu to teach him, Joshu does so in the most
direct way he knows. He tells him to go and wash his bowl.

This can be taken in a literal sense and a more symbolic
sense. On the literal level, Joshu's answer is simple and
pragmatic. In a comment on this koan, Zen master Mumon
thought this was so blindingly obvious that he likened the
monk to a dunce who went searching for a fire with a lighted
lantern! Joshu instructs the monk to do what needs to be done.
If the bowl is still dirty from breakfast, then it needs washing.
And if you're able to wash the bowl with complete attention
and presence, then the sense of "you" doing the "washing"
will eventually blend together – you and the act of washing
will become one. When you do that, there stops being a
distinction between you and the whole universe. Joshu was
encouraging him to find this truth.

On the more symbolic level, the little bits of sticky rice left
in the bowl (which are numerous if, like me, your chopstick
skills leave a lot to be desired) represent those elements in us
that are still stuck – ideas we're still holding on to and things

we haven't let go of yet. Washing the bowl therefore means doing *sange*. It means taking a hard look at our life and what we might still be holding on to or resisting in some way. The act of washing is the act of letting go and aligning the way we live our lives more closely with our true nature.

But *sange* isn't something we do only once. The process of *sange* continues throughout our onward spiritual journey as we see the effects of our past deeds more clearly and learn to let go more completely. Gradually we fine-tune our lives to be more and more in accord with our own truth. My Zen teacher once explained that first you learn to put down all the stuff you've picked up through the years of your life – the resentments, opinions, habits, blame, the hopes for things to go "your way", and so on. Then you learn how not to pick them up in the first place. The true answer to the koan is to live your life without regret and with an intention to be as aware and kind as possible.

As you do this, you become more truly yourself. Gradually, you'll find that you feel more and more at home in this world, wherever you are physically. There'll be a deepening sense of contentment – whether you're listening to your uncle rant on about the state of the economy, or you've just discovered that your colleague is using your favourite coffee mug, or you're quietly sitting on the beach at sunset. This brings us to the final koan we'll look at: as the Buddha was walking with his congregation one day, he pointed to the ground with his finger and said: "This spot is good to build a sanctuary." At that moment, Indra, the Emperor of the Gods, took a blade of grass, stuck it in the ground, and said: "The sanctuary is built." The Buddha smiled.[33]

The koan encourages us to realize that our sanctuary is actually here, right now – in this moment and place. This sanctuary is the knowledge that whatever happens, however spiteful or irritating people can be, and however painful or uncomfortable we feel, it's okay. What starts off as a difficult person we just wish wasn't there, becomes our Buddha-of-the-moment – a Buddha that can ultimately teach us how to find our sanctuary of contentment wherever we are in the world, in whatever situation we find ourselves. And our sanctuary is something that will be continuously remade and refined as we journey through life.

But we never need to feel like we're doing this alone. When we look around, we realize our sanctuary is actually made of our loved ones. Holding up one pillar might be your parents, holding up another pillar might be your partner or best friend, and the roof – that might be your whole friendship network or spiritual community. After all, we already know that a virtuous person is never alone, and that admirable friendship, admirable companionship, admirable camaraderie is the whole of the holy life.

I wish you many wonderfully troublesome Buddhas.

SUMMARY OF APPROACHES WE'VE ENCOUNTERED

Despite the fact that the foregoing accounts are all set in different environments and revolve around different kinds of people, we can see a range of common approaches in regard to how each person dealt with their troublesome Buddhas. I've pulled out a handful below, but maybe you see others – or see them in a different way.

Realizing that perception and reality are two different things

We can never know the full complexity of the situation, including what others think and feel. It's important to appreciate that what we perceive, and the judgements and opinions we form based on that information, will always be biased and incomplete.

Stop believing your thoughts

A corollary of the first point is that our thoughts do not always reflect reality. Don't believe all your thoughts! Accept you might be wrong sometimes. Trying to work things out intellectually is not always helpful.

Turning the lamp around

This means examining your thoughts, feelings, emotions opinions and habits; enquiring with open honesty into where your difficulty, frustration or anger is coming from. It means being curious rather than critical.

Tuning into physical sensations

Noticing your physical sensations can be of help in a variety of ways.

- Because sensations can only be felt in the present moment, becoming aware of how we physically feel (dropping our awareness into the body) helps us disentangle ourselves from the complicated storylines of who did what and what might happen next. The act of noticing interrupts our habitual reactions and provides a space to be with things as they are.
- Physical sensations are much simpler than thoughts, memories and ideas – even if they can sometimes be uncomfortable or painful. It's therefore easier to accept what's happening when we tune into the level of our sensations. Furthermore, every emotion has an epicentre somewhere physically in the body, which we can find if we listen closely enough. When you bring your attention to a discomfort or pain in the body, it changes, and that can change the corresponding emotion.
- Sensations can become clear indicators of when we're resisting or pushing people away – for example, the tension or stiffness in the muscles, or discomfort in the belly.

- Sometimes, anger with a difficult person can become a window or opening into a level of deeper, repressed anger and other emotions that have their roots somewhere in our past. Allowing these emotions, feeling them and expressing them can help us get in touch with these deeper layers of feeling and thus gradually unwind their power or influence over us.

Nari kiru

This Japanese phrase means "to become one with". When you feel or sense something, avoid trying to look back at yourself like a CCTV camera, monitoring or judging how you appear. Try to fully embody it – feel it or do it 100 per cent.

Let our feelings inform our actions

When we truly, honestly and openly accept how we're feeling, then we can let the full gamut of those feelings inform our actions. It might be that underneath the seething anger we find a quiet, previously unacknowledged seed of compassion. Noticing it might have a dramatic influence on how we respond to a difficult person.

Letting go

Letting go is a key part of the practice of mindfulness and Zen. In addition to what I've mentioned already, we can:

- Let go of blaming. This means taking responsibility for our own feelings and, as Jung put it, "withdrawing the projection of our own shadow onto others".
- Let go of wanting or wishing someone to be a certain way. When you wish someone was different, this is living in a fantasy world. Giving up on your wish may mean you end up having to grieve the loss of the person you wanted them to be.

Finding the steadiness that's always there

Even when the surface of the ocean is rough and stormy, you don't have to go far beneath that before things are much calmer. It can be like that in life too. Even when life feels turbulent, confusing or unsettled, try to find that sense of stillness, steadiness and silence that's always there underneath. Regularly practising meditation can help with this.

Persevering with the relationship

It's easy to jump to conclusions about a person after a flash of initial feelings and judgements. But, with time, new aspects and perspectives may come into view which might change your opinion or soften the difficulties. However, persevering with a relationship isn't always appropriate, so it's important to be discerning here.

Compassion and kindness

Being compassionate means having the willingness to see and accept the suffering in the world – in others and yourself. Developing an intention to be kind, open and friendly can dramatically reshape the nature of a troublesome relationship.

Seeing their Buddha-nature

This is about seeing beyond the surface layers of suffering and the various psychological protection mechanisms that might be at play in your troublesome person to find that which is common to all beings – perceiving them as not separate from you. Some call this seeing their inner light or true nature.

Realizing when you need help from others

None of us have all the skills and strength to deal with every difficult situation life throws at us. It's imperative that we reach out for help from others when necessary – be that a friend or a professional (such as a psychotherapist).

Not putting people on a pedestal

Idolizing people or wanting them to be more than they actually are can cause difficulty on both sides of the relationship. We will inevitably be disappointed and end up suffering.

As we've seen, all these approaches can be used over the whole spectrum of troublesomeness, from the slightly stressful to the tragic. Please don't try to remember them so you can apply them like a recipe. That would be trying to work things out intellectually – which, as we know, isn't always that helpful! Read them and let them percolate from your conscious mind down into your being. Like that, we're informing our unconscious so that, when the time arises, we might just take a different, wiser and more compassionate approach with a troublesome person than we might have before. As my Zen teacher has often told me: "Get the understanding, then chuck it over your shoulder and move onto the next thing."

ENDNOTES

1   Mitsunaga Kakudo (1996), quoted in: Covell, S G,
    "Learning to Persevere: The Popular Teachings of
    Tendai Ascetic", *Japanese Journal of Religious Studies*,
    2004, 31, *255–287*

2   Jiyu-Kennett, PTNH, *Zen is Eternal Life*, Shasta
    Abbey Press, California, 1999, p.251

3   Thanissaro Bhikkhu, tr, *Madhupindika Sutta: The Ball
    of Honey* (MN 18), 1999, www.accesstoinsight.org/
    tipitaka/mn/mn.018.than.html

4   Schloegl, I, tr, *The Zen Teaching of Rinzai*, Shambhala,
    Berkeley, 1975, p.76

5   Literally "group Zen study". You can read more
    in: Skinner, J D, ed, *The Zen Character: Life, Art and
    Teachings of Zen Master Shinzan Miyamae*, Zenways
    Press, London, 2015

6   Porges, S W, *The Polyvagal Theory: Neurophysiological
    Foundations of Emotions, Attachment, Communication,
    and Self-regulation*, W W Norton & Company., New
    York, 2011

7   *Analects 4.25*

8   For more on the social engagement system, see
        Porges, *The Polyvagal Theory*

9   Bowlby, J, "The nature of the child's tie to his
        mother", *International Journal of Psychoanalysis,*
        1958, 39, 350–373; Hazan, C and Shaver, P,
        "Romantic love conceptualized as an attachment
        process", *Journal of Personality and Social Psychology,*
        1987, 52, 511–524

10   If you're interested to read more in this area, I'd
        recommend the following insightful book: Miller, A,
        *The Drama of the Gifted Child: The Search for the True
        Self,* Basic Books, New York 1997

11   From Dogen's *Shobogenzo,* global.sotozen-net.or.jp/
        common_html/zuimonki/01-06.html

12   Paraphrased from: Merton, T, tr, *The Way of Chuang
        Tzu,* New Directions, New York, 1965

13   The noble eightfold path is one of the Buddha's
        primary teachings on developing awakening: right/
        proper view, right intention, right speech, right
        action, right livelihood, right effort, right mindfulness
        and right concentration

14   Thanissaro Bhikkhu, tr, *Upaddha Sutta: Half (of the
        Holy Life)* (SN 45.2), *2013,* www.accesstoinsight.org/
        tipitaka/sn/sn45/sn45.002.than.html

15   The Dalai Lama, *Ethics for the New Millennium,*
        Riverhead Books, New York, 2001

16   A commitment to live while avoiding killing, lying,
        stealing, sexual misconduct, consuming intoxicants,
        dwelling on mistakes, boasting or belittling others,
        being stingy, harbouring anger or slandering the
        Buddhist path

17   Part of the noble eightfold path, the others being
        right view, right action, right livelihood, right effort,
        right mindfulness and right concentration

18   Boundless loving kindness, compassion, sympathetic
        joy and peace, introduced to the mainstream

of Rinzai Zen practice by Zen master Torei Enji (1721–92)

19 Thanissaro Bhikkhu, tr, *Samajivina Sutta: Living in Tune* (AN 4.55), 2013, www.accesstoinsight.org/tipitaka/an/an04/an04.055.than.html

20 https://www.ramdass.org/ram-dass-quotes/

21 His autobiographical story is described in: Waddell, N, tr, *The Unborn: The Life and Teachings of Zen Master Bankei,* North Point Press, New York, 2002; and Skinner, J D, *Practical Zen: Meditation and Beyond,* Singing Dragon Press, London, 2017

22 Waddell, N, tr, *Beating the Cloth Drum: Letters of Zen Master Hakuin,* Shambhala, Berkeley, 2012

23 Quote from: MT, *A Sponsorship Guide for All Twelve-Step Programs,* PT Publications, WEST PALM BEACH, FL, 1995

24 This is expressed in: Nyanaponika Thera, tr, *Alagaddupama Sutta* (MN 22), 2006, www.accesstoinsight.org/lib/authors/nyanaponika/wheel048.html#section-13

25 Thanissaro Bhikkhu, tr, *Magandiya Sutta,* 1994, www.accesstoinsight.org/tipitaka/kn/snp/snp.4.09.than.html; fakebuddhaquotes.com/people-with-opinions-just-go-around-bothering-each-other/

26 See "The Raft Parable" in: Nyanaponika Thera, tr, *Alagaddupama Sutta* (MN 22), 2006, www.accesstoinsight.org/lib/authors/nyanaponika/wheel048.html#section-13

27 fakebuddhaquotes.com/dont-keep-searching-for-the-truth-just-let-go-of-your-opinions/

28 See case 2 in the *Hekiganroku (Blue Cliff Record)*

29 The origins of this phrase most likely have their roots in the *Ummonroku (Record of Ummon).* An equivalent phrase put forward by Torei is: "The cattle of Huai Province eat grain; the horses of Yi Province get full", quoted in: Cleary, T, tr, *The*

Undying Lamp of Zen: The Testament of Zen Master Torei, Shambhala, Berkeley, 2010

30   Waddell, N, tr, *Wild Ivy: The Spiritual Autobiography of Zen Master Hakuin*, Shambhala, Berkeley, 2010

31   The origin of this example comes from case 89 of the *Hekiganroku* (Blue Cliff Record): Ungan asked Dogo: "What does the Bodhisattva of Great Mercy use so many hands and eyes for?" Dogo answered: "It is like a person straightening their pillow with their outstretched hand in the middle of the night."

32   Kübler-Ross, E, *Death: The Final Stage of Growth*, Scribner, New York, 1997

33   Case 4 in the *Shoyoroku*, "The World Honoured One Points to the Ground", translated in: Cleary, T, tr, *Book of Serenity*, Shambhala, Berkeley, 2005

ACKNOWLEDGEMENTS

Firstly I'd like to give a deep bow of gratitude to all the people that have ever annoyed or irritated me or pressed my buttons. You have been my teachers.

I'd also like to say a huge thank you to my Zen teacher, Daizan Skinner Roshi, who runs the Zenways *sangha* in London, UK, of which I've been a member for more than ten years. I'd like to thank my wife, Johanna Barclay, for being so supportive and patient and for her stimulating conversations on the topics in this book. Thank you also to my author-friend Livi Michael for her comments on earlier versions of this book.

I'd like to acknowledge and thank the fantastic team at Watkins that have made this book a reality. Thanks especially to my commissioning editor Fiona Robertson for believing in it from the word go.

Finally I'd like to thank all the various members of the Zenways *sangha* who have contributed interviews, examples and inspiration for this book, including Hogetsu Bärndal, Sophie Barraclough, Pete Jion Cherry, Jason Christopher, Penny Seizan Clay, Sean Rinryu Collins, Maxine Craig, Lizzie Daiki Davison, Ed Evans, Sarah Daisho Holt, Matt Shinkai Kane, Mia Livingstone, April Gensei Mannino, Mary Hartley Daikan Platt, Pablo Mokusei Lopez Pleguezuelo, Alla Omelchenko, Chris Owen and Noriko Yamasaki. This book is a testament to the depth of your practice.

WATKINS

Sharing Wisdom Since 1893

The story of Watkins began in 1893, when scholar of esotericism John Watkins founded our bookshop, inspired by the lament of his friend and teacher Madame Blavatsky that there was nowhere in London to buy books on mysticism, occultism or metaphysics. That moment marked the birth of Watkins, soon to become the publisher of many of the leading lights of spiritual literature, including Carl Jung, Rudolf Steiner, Alice Bailey and Chögyam Trungpa.

Today, the passion at Watkins Publishing for vigorous questioning is still resolute. Our stimulating and groundbreaking list ranges from ancient traditions and complementary medicine to the latest ideas about personal development, holistic wellbeing and consciousness exploration. We remain at the cutting edge, committed to publishing books that change lives.

DISCOVER MORE AT:

www.watkinspublishing.com

Read our blog

Watch and listen to
our authors in action

Sign up to
our mailing list

We celebrate conscious, passionate, wise and happy living.
Be part of that community by visiting

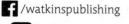 /watkinspublishing   @watkinswisdom

 /watkinsbooks   @watkinswisdom